More Love

For Ben, Caleb, Barnaby, Andrew and Elijah

All words in italic are the exact writing of Elizabeth Prentiss as recorded in letters and journals collected by her husband, George. These were published as a collection called 'The life and letters of Elizabeth Prentiss.'

More Love

Elizabeth Prentiss

Claire Williams

CF4•K

10 9 8 7 6 5 4 3 2 1
Copyright © 2019 Claire Williams

Paperback ISBN: 978-1-5271-0299-6
epub ISBN: 978-1-5271-0347-4
mobi ISBN: 978-1-5271-0348-1

Published by
Christian Focus Publications, Geanies House, Fearn, Tain,
Ross-shire, IV20 1TW, Scotland, U.K.
www.christianfocus.com
email: info@christianfocus.com

Printed and bound by Nørhaven, Denmark
Cover design by Daniel van Straaten

Scripture quotations are from The Holy Bible, English Standard Version, copyright © 2001 by Crossway Bibles, a publishing ministry of Good News Publishers. Used by permission. All rights reserved. ESV Text Edition: 2011.

This book is based mostly on true episodes in the character's life. However, sometimes the author has created incidents that are not directly biographical, but that would have happened in families at the time period. Occasionally the author has had to make assumptions about some background details regarding travel. All of this helps the reader to understand the cultural differences between Elizabeth Prentiss' time and ours. Dialogue is on the whole fictionalised unless it is made clear that it is a direct quote. Sometimes what was a conversation in real life has been changed to a letter for ease of narrative.

All rights reserved. No part of this publication may be reproduced, stored in a retrieval system, or transmitted, in any form, by any means, electronic, mechanical, photocopying, recording or otherwise without the prior permission of the publisher or a licence permitting restricted copying. In the U.K. such licences are issued by the Copyright Licensing Agency, Saffron House, 6-10 Kirby Street, London, EC1 8TS. www.cla.co.uk

Contents

A Girl called Lizzie..7

Growing up with Christ 15

Teaching the Girls in Richmond......................25

Blessings and Sadnesses............................... 41

Writing, Writing, Writing............................. 53

Letters and Holidays.................................... 63

Life in Switzerland...................................... 79

Louisa and the War...................................... 95

At Home with Lizzie.................................. 101

Stepping Heavenward................................. 111

Joy in the Hard Times................................. 119

Thinking Further Topics.............................. 122

Elizabeth Prentiss Timeline........................... 134

A Girl called Lizzie

A piercing wail broke forth from the upstairs room. The new baby was announcing herself to the world! Edward Payson, the much loved pastor and preacher, glanced up in the direction of the sound. He smiled to himself. His new daughter, was a delight and very much hoped for by his wife who longed for another girl. The house hummed with happiness and hope but also rejoicing, the home was delighting in the blessing God had poured upon them. Edward turned back to his letter that he had been writing at his desk.

'Louisa and the babe continue as well as we could desire. Truly, my cup runs over with blessings.'

Edward wrote to his mother. His new daughter had been called Elizabeth. She had been born the day before at about three o'clock in the afternoon in the middle of October, right in the glories of a New England autumn. The leaves on the trees outside their home were turning more colours than anyone could name, the world was looking beautiful. Everything was

More Love

declaring the wonders of God and Edward was rejoicing alongside creation.

The house that Edward and his family lived in was wonderful, with large windows that faced onto the tree that grew out of the front of the house. It had a good number of rooms and despite being a formal style as many homes were around there, it was warm and welcoming. The family received many visitors, calling upon their beloved pastor for all his kindness, wisdom and insight.

Elizabeth lay in her bed looking out of the window. Elizabeth spent her early years under the love and guidance of this kind and wise man. It meant that at six years old she was a happy, inquisitive little girl, who enjoyed looking out of a window, gazing intensely at squirrels. She was so happy when she looked at nature and the world around her. Her very slight frame trembled with a chill that was made worse by her being ill, again. She was often ill and this made her frustrated. Her family, who loved and adored her and were loved and adored fiercely back, would sit with her and read to her or talk whilst she recovered. Nobody was sitting with her at the moment though, just her and the squirrel. Elizabeth sighed. The squirrel nibbled a nut it had found and its fluffy tail wrapped around it like a coat. It had a drey further up the tree and Elizabeth had been watching it during the time that she was ill. They were friends! She quite hoped that she would see some baby squirrels at some point. Elizabeth loved all of nature and thought that she lived in the best, most beautiful place in the world.

'Father! Father!' Elizabeth came barrelling into the room, without pausing to knock like she was supposed to. She was busy thinking about something else.

'Goodness, my Elizabeth, you are a whirlwind. Whatever is going on?' Elizabeth's father turned round in his chair, stopping work on his sermon. He had seen unexpected visitors this morning who had wanted his advice and now he had another unexpected visitor, although he wasn't quite sure Elizabeth was after advice!

'Sorry, Papa, I realised that I hadn't seen you all day, then I realised that I wanted to tell you about school today, and the poem I've written, and the new squirrel I saw, and, and ...'

'Woah, calm down, my Lizzie! I don't think I can keep up with you!' He looked at her with his beautiful brown eyes that were filled with love for his passionate daughter. She was wild with fun and frolic and nobody could help but adore her. In return, she adored her father and spent as much time as she possibly could with him. This was his pleasure and delight.

'Sorry.' Elizabeth caught her breath and looked at him. 'Are you quite better now from your illness?' Her face showed concern as she examined him carefully, all her haste forgotten now.

'Yes, I am quite better, fully recovered, praise God.' Elizabeth grinned.

More Love

'Yes, praise God! He always looks after us, just like you tell me.'

'Indeed, and now I have something to show you. Come over to the window.' Elizabeth looked curious, her natural need to learn and know what was going on piqued.

Edward stood up from his Bible, carefully placing a ribbon in his place and closing it. He walked across the wooden boarded floor and looked out of the window into another glorious Maine autumn. The house grandly stood, as many New England houses did, looking out into the town with the sea just beyond. The horizon was clear and the sun was dappled through the leaves that still clung onto the trees.

'Now, watch this, we shall have snow early this year!' He reached out of his pocket a handful of pieces of paper and opened the window. He held out his hand to Elizabeth and nodded his head. Elizabeth tilted her head curiously, not sure what he meant. Then it dawned on her. She bounced on her toes, and grabbed a handful of paper. With a delighted squeal she threw the paper out of the window, it fluttered down, just like real snow. It was lovely !

'Oh, how wonderful, Papa! Aren't you clever! Did you think of this just for me?' Elizabeth's face shone with happiness, her father was so kind and thoughtful, even though he was so busy.

'Of course I did, sweetheart. I knew that you would like it.' Her father's face paled a little, and he began to cough.

Elizabeth Prentiss

'Sit down, father! You are tired! I will fetch Mother.' Elizabeth helped her father back to his chair and dashed from the room. This was a memory, of her father making it snow, that she would treasure in her heart forever.

Elizabeth sat in the pew looking straight ahead. Her eyes were clouded with tears and her mind clouded with confusion. Her father was addressing the church, he had stopped being well enough to preach sermons a while ago, but had been determined to stand before them one last time. Elizabeth wasn't sure she could endure it. Later she would look back at this time as her father's last sermon, age only eight she could hardly take it all in at the time.

'I shall never behold another spring ...' He began solemnly but kindly. Elizabeth choked on a sob and buried her head in her handkerchief. Her big sister Louisa held her hand tightly. Her brothers sitting further down the row looked pale and drawn but bravely carried on watching their father. Elizabeth couldn't even look at Mother. She didn't want to see her being brave and heartbroken all at once. Her father had tuberculosis, consumption, any number of words described what he had and for once Elizabeth didn't really care to think of them. They had just moved into a smaller house that her mother could manage when her father had gone. Her father had arranged all of this so that he could be present in their future home, to leave a

More Love

little of himself in the place they would live, so that they didn't feel they had lost him and their memories of him all at once. He was incredibly thoughtful in this way.

Some weeks passed and Elizabeth's father was not even well enough to go out of the house, far less to preach. But life continued even from the four walls of the Payson home. The girls sat together reading, Louisa was engrossed in Hebrew translation, something for which she had a remarkable gift. There were high hopes of Louisa from some of the congregation, that her mind would be used for many marvellous things. Elizabeth was impressed with her sister and with her father. Even though Rev. Payson was seriously ill, he made time to meet another couple from the confines of his sickbed. His endeavour was to see as many people as he could, to impart God's wisdom to them in his final months. Elizabeth looked up from the book that she was almost finished with and reflected on a conversation that she had had with her father earlier that day. He had been propped up in his bed, the fire in the hearth was going well, the crackle and pop of the wood a reassuring sound and distracting her from the wheezing her father was making.

'My dear Elizabeth. What a wonderful girl you are. I am delighted in you, do you know that?' He looked at her calmly. Elizabeth smiled at him.

'And I you, Father.'

'I have peace in my soul. God's will is all I need, that is where true happiness is, to trust God. God has

Elizabeth Prentiss

removed from me one blessing after another, but each time he has filled up the space left behind. I can see heaven Elizabeth, *its glories beam upon me, its breezes fan me, its odours are wafted to me, its sounds strike upon my ear and its spirit is breathed into my heart.*'

When the time came the grief hit hard, but God sent Elizabeth comfort. She lay in her bed and sobbed into her pillow. It was sodden with her tears. Her mother had sat with her for a good while that evening, stroking her hair and praying with her daughter. Elizabeth, frustrated and angry still remembered the funeral with vivid clarity. She read the note that her father had asked to be pinned to his chest in the coffin, '*Remember the words which I spake unto you while I was yet present with you*'. Elizabeth hoped that she would always remember her Father, every last detail. She remembered clearly another time when she dashed into her father's room to find him prostrate on the floor in prayer. Now it was more common to hear her mother's footsteps as she walked to the spare room and shut the door, to speak with God. Elizabeth knew firmly that this was the way to live, to never stop speaking to the Heavenly Father who loved her. Meanwhile, she missed her earthly father with a hurt so real that it felt like a huge tear in her heart. She turned her face back into her pillow, he would never read her a bedtime story again.

Growing up with Christ

'I don't doubt that you can do it,' Elizabeth's mother patiently explained. Elizabeth was just twelve years old and extremely determined, when she was in the right mood!

'Are you sure? I'm certain that I can.' Elizabeth held on tightly to the book she had just received from her mother.

'I am certain. When you are determined to do something, you usually manage it!'

Elizabeth glanced down at the catechism in her hands. The question and answers that it contained would help her to learn and always have with her the truths about God.

'I am a bit cross with myself for feeling so uninterested last week, but I am glad that I am interested now.'

'Yes, well, that has been the case in the past, my passionate daughter! God understands, and so do I. Memorising the catechism is an excellent idea. All the beliefs of Christianity are contained within it, and it

More Love

is written to be easy to remember. If you are asked the question, you can remember the answer. Shall we do the first one?' Elizabeth nodded eagerly, she was raring to go.

'What is the chief end of man?' Elizabeth's mother asked her clearly, without looking at the book.

'Um ...' Elizabeth paused, searching for the answer, 'Oh, I remember! To glorify God and enjoy him forever!' Elizabeth danced across the kitchen floor as she celebrated her success. 'I knew I could do it!'

'Good,' said Elizabeth's mother. 'What rule has God given us, to direct us so that we may glorify and enjoy him?'

'Hmm, Scripture!' Elizabeth squeaked.

'Yes, but what is the full answer?'

'Right. It's ...' Elizabeth paused for a moment and tugged at her plait while she thought. 'The word of God, which is contained in the Scriptures, is the only rule to direct us how we should glorify and enjoy him.'

'Last one for now, how did God create man?' Elizabeth's mother smiled, she had asked her one from a different place in the catechism, just to test Elizabeth.

'Oh, Mother! You thought you could catch me out! God created man male and female, after his own image.' Elizabeth smiled, slightly smugly.

Not all of Elizabeth's days were spent memorising – sometimes her health anchored her to the bed where she barely had the energy to look at squirrels far less

Elizabeth Prentiss

remember catechisms. The tree outside this bedroom window didn't even seem to have a squirrel in it, not that Elizabeth had tried to look very carefully. It was full of lush green leaves, dancing in the gentle spring breeze. Mrs Payson sat by her daughter's bedside as she tried to interest the young girl in the antics of two little songbirds on the tree outside. Elizabeth would usually have chuckled at their silly antics, especially the newly fledged, fluffy, little ones who still expected their parents to feed them every minute. However, today was not like a normal day, today Elizabeth was really very ill. Mrs Payson sat by her bedside, her journal in her lap.

'Elizabeth remains gravely ill. I have never seen such an ill child. I had feared that she would not emerge from her fever and that she would shortly be reunited with our Lord and Saviour. Nonetheless, the good Doctor assures me that despite how it seems, apart from all our expectations, Elizabeth has turned a corner and we can reasonably expect her return to full health. I am, of course, delighted and immensely relieved. All the household has worried and prayed without ceasing. I have almost lost the feeling in my toes and fingers from the time spent in the cold spare room entreating the Lord for my daughter's sake. I am led to believe, and believe it most strongly, that he has spared her to be used in his service.'

Elizabeth stirred and mumbled a bit. Her mother wiped her forehead again and swept her messy hair off of her face and away from her eyes. They flickered open.

More Love

'Mother?' she groaned.

'Yes, my darling, I'm right here.'

'Am I to recover?' She sounded stronger even then, she hadn't spoken clearly for a number of days.

'Yes, God has seen fit to spare you and us, the doctor says that you shall be quite well and racing around in a fit of passion very soon. Help us all!' Her mother spoke gently, stroking her girl's head all the while.

'I am grateful, I feel as though God is closer today than I have ever known.'

'And yet, my sweet girl, he is close and always has been. Rest again, my darling . You'll soon be well.'

And she was. In only a few weeks she was back in the family pew. And not long after that there was yet another reason for celebration. Not only was she returned to the pew she was joining the church.

Elizabeth stood with a straight back and an extremely serious look upon her face. The church congregation were all smiling at her as the pastor solemnly shook the young girl's hand.

'We are delighted, Elizabeth Payson, to welcome you into our church as a member. We have heard your confession of faith and we shall watch you grow in the Lord with joy.' He smiled at the intense young girl of twelve who stood before him. He looked forward to watching her grow up.

Elizabeth probably thought she was quite grown up already. She and her friends certainly grappled with the deeper questions of life. Elizabeth and her

Elizabeth Prentiss

friend loved to watch the boats drift in and out of the harbour, floating as if they had no intention of rushing, all the while the girls would sit and talk about their favourite books. Perhaps it was the beautiful spring day with the haze that covered the horizon that meant everyone wanted to just enjoy it, rather than rushing about. They often chose to sit on a large marble slab in the cemetery and just let the world go by. Elizabeth chewed on a piece of grass as she shared the details of her new book ...

'Well,' Elizabeth began, 'it is about Miss Susanna Anthony, a woman who suffered so terribly but so beautifully.'

'Why, I wish I knew, does God who commands all things, allow these sufferings to happen? I do not believe that it is right!' Her friend puffed out her breath crossly.

'Well, we can't understand it, but I have been thinking this might be God's way of preparing his children for very high degrees of service on earth, or happiness in heaven.' Elizabeth replied quite sweetly and with a deep contentment. She really did believe it. Her friend thought for a moment.

'I don't think, dear Elizabeth, that I shall ever forget that now that you have explained it to me.'

Elizabeth aged eighteen sat at her desk in her new room and wrote in her journal. Elizabeth certainly was growing up you could see it physically, but also spiritually.

More Love

I sincerely dislike this 'pumpkin house'. It is ugly and of such an unpleasant colour that I feel as though I should hate it forever. However, the view is beautiful, all the way out over Casco Bay and the White Mountains. My love for all that God has made is stronger than ever, the natural world around me is so splendid and the pumpkin house does at least provide a remarkable access to it. I find myself running, skipping and hopping and I even climbed a fence! I have decided I am not ladylike and I am not a lady! I spent four solid hours walking in our little garden, it was a delight and I adored it.

'It is autumn now and we have quit the pumpkin house for good!' celebrated Elizabeth as she hauled one last heavy case of things towards their new home.

'Elizabeth you are prone to ingratitude' reprimanded her mother, 'just like with the magazines that want you to write for them and you tell them no!'

'Mother, darling Mother, that is not ingratitude! I cannot write for them, I am not able enough for that. Just the other day I read the "Pickwick Papers" and I nearly cried with laughter. How can I write anything ever again when I have read such writing?' Elizabeth declared with feeling.

'Elizabeth,' her mother put down the carpet that she had carried, rolled up, into the house. 'You have been given a gift by God. You can use it to serve him. Your writing is fine, well crafted and brilliant.'

'Mother, you are empowered with the rose tinted spectacles of maternal love!' Elizabeth giggled at the phrase, 'You love me too much!'

'I shall never apologise for it!' Her mother nearly stamped her foot! This was not something that Elizabeth's mother was going to budge on. 'Ah, you give me some worries, my girl.'

'Why?'

'I am worried because you swing from adoring the Lord and showing your young charges in Sunday school about him and leading them to him, from that, to telling me that he is impossible to love.' Her mother furrowed her brow with some concern as she faced her impetuous youngest daughter, with her skirts slightly dusty from moving and her hair falling out of place.

'Mother, I despair of myself, I do. I feel so strongly one moment that I love him more than I can bear, more than I can contain, then another moment, barely a day later, I fall into a pit of not knowing him at all. How can I be sure? How can I be confident in the faith that you and father have?'

Mrs Payson grasped her daughter's hand, it had callouses from all the mending they did for Elizabeth's brothers who grew and tore and generally ruined their clothes. It was a gentle hand, a kind one, and right now it squeezed Elizabeth's tightly.

'You must be content. You can be content. The Lord is not far off, sometimes trusting in our emotions leads

More Love

us down a false path. It is not what we feel, more what we know. You will be sure soon.'

'Mother, I do so hope so. Now, where are all the boxes? I need some more for my books will not fit in the ones that I already have and there is all of the hats in my room to think of too! When we move to Cumberland Street we must have hats! And books, of course!'

Elizabeth sighed and looked around the room that she had not long ago decorated and arranged herself. The move to Cumberland Street had caused an unexpected opportunity and Elizabeth had delighted in it.

'Miss Payson?' A young girl of about ten called out from her place in the circle of chairs that the thirty or so young girls were seated at.

'Oh,' Elizabeth startled. 'I'm sorry girls, I lost my train of thought. Where was I? Who can tell me?' She glanced fondly around the group, taking the opportunity to check if they had been listening. Thirty hands raised into the air!

'Goodness, all of you know! How marvellous, okay Julia, perhaps you can tell me?'

'You were telling us about the time that you spent feeling ever so guilty about having a temper, or that is what you have called it?' The girl looked suddenly unsure at accusing her teacher of being short tempered.

'Yes, Julia, don't look so worried. I am freely confessing to you that I spent four long months in misery at the state of myself. I had been trying to pray, trying to please the Lord, trying to improve myself in any way that I could. I was so aware of my sin, so confounded with the love of one who would not abandon one such as me!' The girls sat, rapt, listening to this story in between their lessons about literature and poetry. Most of them loved Elizabeth so much that they could scarcely believe their teacher ever felt so desperate.

'Girls, I could not work my way to the Lord. I could not present myself unblemished. It would not work. Instead I listened to a man wiser than I. He taught at church, you may remember, that Christ saves even the worst of us. I realised then that I need do nothing other than praise and adore him. So I now do and the freedom from anxiety and despair is complete! I am happy to say that I am *daily nearer God!*'

Teaching the Girls in Richmond

Elizabeth stepped down from the train and pushed the door shut with her elbow her suitcases bashing against her legs as she did so. It didn't quite close and another passenger leaned over and gave it a hard shove for her. She was twenty-two years old now, growing both in stature and in faithfulness to God.

'Thank you.' Elizabeth smiled into the darkness, unable to see the face of her helper. She looked all around her.

'It is *dark as pitch*,' Elizabeth huffed. She was excited about her new adventure but also nervous. Leaving behind all that she knew to start something different was exhilarating, she was so glad that she was going to be starting with her good friend Louisa. They were to share a bedroom, something that was so familiar to Elizabeth after sharing with her sister for a long time, that it would remind her of being at home.

The stars were shining, but they were so, so small and the moon was waning and not casting any light. This was quite the adventure! The bridge between this

More Love

stop and her actual stop had burnt down. The train terminated here, whether anyone wanted it to, or not! The difficulty was that her stop was the next one and Mr Persico's school, where Elizabeth was due to start teaching, was a ten minute walk after that. Elizabeth stared into the darkness. The station master was waving all the passengers into a line and shouting something at them. Elizabeth edged closer.

'Everyone this way!' he bellowed, 'Madam, watch your step, this path to the next station.' Elizabeth looked to where the station master was pointing. There, at intervals, were burning bonfires serving to mark the way towards their journey's end. The path was narrow, it turned and twisted up a hill. It was rather steep, more steep than Elizabeth's usual walking places. Some of the other women in the party of travellers started muttering amongst themselves about how hard it looked. Elizabeth determined to not do that! She grabbed her two suitcases in her gloved hands, straightened up her back and started towards the first bonfire. Thank goodness that Richmond, where the school was located, was not cold. Mr Persico had moved to the warmer climate for the health of his ailing wife and had started the school. Elizabeth was of a mind that this hike would have been much more of a challenge had it been faced in either the warmth that the daytime would have provided or the cold that happened in the winter. But as it was, this was a great adventure and she was excited.

Elizabeth Prentiss

Approaching the final bonfire Elizabeth glanced around her. The lights of Richmond were in view and her arms, although they felt like they were a few inches longer, did not ache so much. The worst pain was still in her heart at leaving her dear family home. Her mother! Oh, how she was to miss her mother. However, she would not be alone, of that she was certain. On the horizon Elizabeth could see a couple waving to her, she looked behind her in case they were for someone else, but no, it was her.

'Miss Payson ! Miss Payson! We are delighted to see you! Oh, how tired you must be from walking!' Mr and Mrs Persico were all beaming smiles and happiness.

'Hello, I am pleased to meet you,' Elizabeth said, perhaps a bit quietly, she was suddenly tired and homesick. They climbed into the transport and it started to move.

'As are we, so pleased. We will take you to the school and show you to your room, or perhaps you would like something to eat?' Mr Persico seemed like he was one who liked to talk!

'Thank you, you are so kind, I think, if I may, I should like to go to my room.' Elizabeth was quite wearied and ready to sleep. They arrived in front of the large house that served as the school. It had three floors and across it were a number of large windows. The front door was heavy and sheltered by an ornate porch, Elizabeth couldn't make out much more of the details, it was too dark and late. The Persicos showed

27

More Love

her into the house and Mrs Persico walked her up to her room. Elizabeth didn't even take the time to light her light, she flung off her shoes, placed her cases upon the floor and fell onto the bed.

The next day dawned, the sun streaming into the window as Elizabeth hadn't shut the curtains the night before. Elizabeth rubbed her eyes and looked around in disappointment. The room was old, her bed was near the window, the other bed, which her friend Louisa was to use, up against the far wall. The wall itself was white but had clearly once been blue as underneath the peeling white paint there was blue paint peeking out. The floor had no carpet, unlike Elizabeth's room at home, and the wind blew through the frames of the windows implying many a cold night to come. Elizabeth gave herself a little shake. This was not the time to wallow in her surroundings. She was here to serve the Lord and to look after the girls that were in her care. She looked over at what would be her desk with the dark wooden shelves above it. She would start getting out her books and setting up home! This would be an adventure. She would be determined to see it as such.

The window panes rattled in the wind. Even though it was not terribly cold during the day, the mornings felt chilly and the darkness was making it hard to see even her own fingers. Elizabeth resolutely pushed back her covers and flung her feet down to the floor with a thump. Her toes inched around, trying to find her shoes. Elizabeth's eyes were adjusting to the dark, she could see the form of her dear friend Louisa buried beneath her blankets on the other bed.

'Louisa.'

Nothing.

'Louisa.'

'Hmmm?' said the lump of blankets.

'Louisa! I am getting up to pray, you have half an hour.' Elizabeth did this every day, she would give her friend an alarm call to get her ready to wake up then tiptoe out into the hallway. There she would sit herself in the deep recess of an old window that looked out over the courtyard and open the scriptures. She began the day the same way every day, reading and praying and dedicating herself and the children in her care to the Lord. She flicked the pages of her worn Bible to the place where the ribbon sat. She had a lot that she wanted to pray and talk to God about and only half an hour to do it in before Louisa would come out to sit in the same place and spend her time with God. Louisa liked being second, it meant she had an extra half hour's sleep and that Elizabeth had warmed up the spot by the window on cold days! They did take turns though. Elizabeth did relish the extra sleep too, but there was something quite wonderful about being the first person up, there was only faint noise from the other early risers from the street at the front of the house, the various folk who had to be up and about early for their work,

More Love

otherwise it was just Elizabeth and God, and that was precious indeed.

The day was begun. Just like most days for Elizabeth her and Louisa walked sedately down the stairs to meet the throng of girls who were anxious to eat their breakfast.

'Good morning, Miss Payson, good morning, Miss Lord,' a number of girls chimed as they made their way towards the dining room.

'Good morning, girls.' Louisa and Elizabeth smiled.

'G-g-good m-m-morning.' A little girl walked past and stumbled over a step as she stumbled over her words.

'Good morning, Ruth,' said Elizabeth with a smile. The little girl looked anxiously up at the two women and hurried towards her place at the table.

'I am concerned about poor Ruth,' Louisa said quietly into Elizabeth's ear.

'As am I,' replied Elizabeth. Ruth stammered when she spoke. It meant that her words didn't come out clearly. Some of the girls were unkind and teased her about it, although not if any teacher were nearby. The little child was painfully shy as a consequence and both Louisa and Elizabeth had worried about her happiness.

'I will give it some more thought,' Elizabeth said as she and Louisa sat down at the broad dining table in the far end of the house. The room contained about

Elizabeth Prentiss

thirty people, including another few teachers who sat with their groups of girls on a second table. The tables were dark oak wood and each girl was expected to sit politely whilst prayers were said and then fetch their breakfast themselves from the serving table at the side of the room. Fortunately the room was big enough for all this to happen and because it had big high ceilings the sound of the girls' voices as they chattered simply floated up and around rather than creating such a din that nobody could think! Today the fire was lit well and the room was warm and cosy. Little Ruth sat quietly at the end of the table that Elizabeth sat on. She was looking at her hands in her lap and her hair braid had fallen so it covered some of her face. She was sitting as if curled up in a world of her own, the girls next to her paid her no heed and Elizabeth was heartbroken for the poor child. Thinking back to her happy childhood home full of love and kindness and looking at this little girl Elizabeth was determined to help.

Such an opportunity arrived sometime later that very day. Ruth was a thin wisp of a girl, who looked always a little too pale. After the first morning classes it was recess time. The girls took a walk around the grounds of the school or sat in small groups chatting, reading and playing. Ruth sat by herself outside. Elizabeth sat with her.

'Hello Ruth. How were this morning's lessons?' Elizabeth smoothed down her skirt and turned her face

More Love

towards the sun, so she wasn't staring at the girl and making the conversation even harder for her.

'G-g-good,' Ruth said. She let out a small noise and Elizabeth startled turned to look at her.

'Oh dear, dear Ruth. Do not cry.' Elizabeth put her arm around Ruth's angular shoulders and pulled her close into her side. The girl leant against her.

'I c-c-can't t-t-talk to anyone,' she wept.

'You are not alone, dear one.'

'Y-y-yes I a-a-am.'

'I have a friend with a similar affliction, I understand it well.' Elizabeth felt a little hand slip into hers, she squeezed it tight. 'We will stick together.' Ruth did not say anything for the tears were falling so hard and fast. Elizabeth felt her own eyes fill as she sat with the sun on her face and the hope of a little girl at her side.

As time passed Elizabeth became well known for being a kind-hearted friend to anyone and an adored teacher to the girls. This was put to the test somewhat with a particularly difficult student.

'Goodness me, what is this?' Elizabeth bent down and picked up a note off of her dinner plate. She glanced either side of her to see if it was mischief from one of the students. Nobody appeared to be watching her. She unfolded the note and flattened it out with her fingers.

'If you are willing to be of service to me, I have a girl who would greatly benefit from your good attention. She is troubled. Could she sleep in your room and dine with you in the hall and spend her time with you?'

Elizabeth Prentiss

It was signed by Mrs Persico. Elizabeth felt a bit glum.

'She will have all my best time,' she muttered to herself, 'and what on earth is the matter that she needs my singular attention like this?' Sighing, perhaps a bit too loudly, Elizabeth continued to think, '*I wanted a place in which to deny myself for the sake of the One who yielded up every comfort for my sake.* This shall be it.' Elizabeth resolved to put aside her desires for time on her own after working to serve this young lady and by doing so serve God who asked of her to care for the little children just as he cared for everyone. Such a sacrifice as Christ had made dying on the cross demanded of Elizabeth every day sacrifices just like this.

'Nannie, you are being obstinate!' The words of one of the other teachers were echoing down the corridor as if a warning to Elizabeth. She ignored it.

'I am not!' The loud and rude shout of a girl too old to be yelling and creating a fuss followed hot on the heels of the teacher's words.

'Hmmm, this is a young lady who does not know how to behave.' Elizabeth was not about to let this pass unattended to, if Nannie was to spend time in Elizabeth's company then she would be loved but not indulged.

'Nannie, my name is Miss Payson. I believe that you owe Miss Thomas an apology.' She did not pause to assess the scene but confidently took immediate

More Love

charge. The girl looked quite surprised, unused to being corrected.

'I'm sorry,' she said, with some genuine contrition, as if shocked into realisation that her behaviour was wrong.

'I understand that you have been having a little trouble at school. Mrs Persico believes coming and staying with me will be of some benefit. I'm very much looking forward to getting to know you better.' Elizabeth smiled warmly at the girl. Nannie hesitated, making up her mind after being told off, then smiled back. Tough love always worked in Elizabeth's experience.

'Well come along then, are those your cases?' Elizabeth turned around and strode out of the door. Nannie hurried along after her.

The put-up bed sat in between Louisa and Elizabeth's own beds. Nannie had placed her bedclothes on it and arranged the blankets so that they were comfortable, this was her nightly routine since she came to stay with Elizabeth. She looked between the two women, quite a look of happiness in her eyes, for it is indeed a privilege to have their time given to her. Elizabeth, however, tutted.

'Do you really read all of these silly novels?' she said, looking at the collection that Nannie had lined up on her part of the shelf when she had moved in. They were some very familiar books, popular amongst some of Nannie's friends. Elizabeth was now quite looking forward to getting rid of them.

Elizabeth Prentiss

'Yes, I do, they are fun.' Nannie was defiant.

'They fill your head with nonsense, Nannie.' Elizabeth countered, 'You are being the same as the other girls in this house who spend their time thinking of nothing else than love stories, and romantic poems, there is much more of worth than these things!'

'Like what?' Nannie wasn't too keen to give up the pleasures of a distracting novel.

'Read the Bible more, learn more about the Lord who loves you. Think about the things that God has called you to do and, well, all of those much more valuable things!'

Nannie considered this, her young face screwed up as she thought.

'If I shall read more of the Bible, then I will be a little more like you, and Miss Louisa?'

'Well, more and more and better and better I should hope.'

'Well then I shall read it, and I shall pray too, I shall pray to God that he might find you an angel to marry, for you are an angel to me for loving me so much when everyone else does not.'

'Now Nannie, where do I start with all that?! I do not desire to marry an angel, I prefer someone who would like me for what I am, which is sometimes not at all perfect, even mischievous! And as for who loves you, well my darling girl, many love you and they desire you to be your best, it is not just me.'

'Well, I shall pray that anyway,' Nannie said stubbornly and she buried her head down into her pillow and yanked the blanket up to her chin, resolutely. She shut her eyes tightly and appeared to begin an in-depth petition. Elizabeth looked at her, amused.

'Ah well, for your sake, may God hear your earnest prayer to him, and mine for you,' murmured Elizabeth quietly.

Elizabeth wiped a sly tear away from her cheek and chastised herself for being so moved by what she read. In her hands lay a letter from Nannie's father. It was addressed to the head of the school, Mr Persico, but Mrs Persico had handed it on for Elizabeth to read. It spoke of the wondrous change in Nannie, how brilliantly the girl now fared. The letter thanked Elizabeth again and again for her work with Nannie, for helping her become so much more happy. Elizabeth smiled as she read it all, thinking back, as she held the letter, over her most recent conversation with the young girl.

'I should think that you would not mind at all if you died tonight,' Nannie said in her characteristically confrontational way of hers. She stared boldly at Elizabeth, as if daring her to be surprised by such a statement. Elizabeth turned her eyes calmly back, as if this young thing could surprise her! Like had met like here! Elizabeth was as fiery and impetuous as she!

'I should not mind in the slightest.'

'Nor would I,' Nannie said with slightly more hesitation in her voice.

Elizabeth Prentiss

'Indeed. Do you think you would be better off than here?'

'Yes, in heaven.'

'Ah, that is certainly true, you are right. Death is not something to be afraid of but welcomed in the right time, for heaven is a wonderful place.'

'I won't take it.'

'Nannie, darling, you are sick, you must take the medicine.' Elizabeth was gentle but firm. Not firm enough!

'No.' Nannie clamped her lips shut and shook her head firmly, somewhat like a toddler.

'Nannie, you don't have a choice, you *must* take this medicine.' Elizabeth dropped the gentle words and looked sternly at her charge who had a fever and was really quite unwell, although not ill enough to do as she was told!

'I really don't like it,' Nannie wavered, looking chastised. 'Oh, okay, if I really must.' She gingerly took the spoon out of Elizabeth's hand and carefully, despite shaking hands because of the fever, managed to put the contents into her mouth. Grimacing, she swallowed. Her eyes looked tired and she placed her head on the pillow. Within mere moments, she was asleep. Elizabeth chuckled. If she believed in magic she might have believed that *must* was a magical word!

A few hours later Elizabeth was stood outside her room with Louisa whilst Nannie, who had woken up

More Love

and had more medicine, slept off the worst of her poor health.

'She thanked me without ceasing for a full ten minutes,' Elizabeth told Louisa.

'For anything in particular?' Louisa was amused.

'For making her mind me, for looking after her, for loving her, for anything and everything. She held so tightly onto my hand that I thought I might loose all feeling in my fingers!'

'How that child has improved herself.' Louisa wondered at it.

'The Lord has seen fit to teach us all through her, I think,' Elizabeth said.

Time passed at the school, Elizabeth was delighted in each adventure she had there. She would have Bible studies full of girls who would hear of the Lord and all his marvellous ways. She attended the occasional party, she spent time with the other teachers and particularly Mrs Persico whom she loved dearly.

There was, however, one development when Elizabeth was a young woman that was particularly special. It happened after Elizabeth had left Richmond and had returned home to be with her mother. Her mother had been sick and Elizabeth had gone back to care for her. During that time she had kept up a regular correspondence of letters with her friend Anna. Anna had been Elizabeth's dear companion for quite some time and Elizabeth's return home had given them a chance to see one another again. As lovely as this was, there was something even more lovely about it, her brother. His name was George!

Elizabeth had strong feelings about getting married. This was, in her mind, not something to be taken lightly. Being a married woman required a great amount of self sacrifice, she would have to give up a lot. Only for a man that she was completely devoted to was this a worthwhile thing. In a time when women often married just because it was expected of them, because everyone thought they should, Elizabeth thought that this was not a good enough reason. Rather she thought that she absolutely must adore and love the man she married. She knew that she was the type of person never to feel things in a small way! She was a very passionate person! She had passionately loved and hated and had strong feelings about all sorts of things. She'd loved her father, Nannie, her mother and of course, God. She'd more than disliked her 'pumpkin house'. There was no chance that falling in love would be anything less than something that took over every part of her. Fortunately, she fell in love with a good, kind, wonderful man, he felt exactly the same. She made an extremely good choice

Elizabeth woke up. It was the 11th of September. Little did she know as she went about getting ready for the day that this was a day that she would mark

More Love

for the rest of her life. However, somewhere across town the man that Elizabeth had recently began to get to know very well was pacing his kitchen floor very nervously. George Prentiss sighed a big sigh, gathered his coat up and straightened his back. Purposefully he strode towards the door. Today he was off to ask a rather wonderful woman a rather big question. He just hoped that she said yes.

Two hours later, she did.

Blessings and Sadnesses

Elizabeth walked into the room where George sat preparing his sermon. He turned around from his desk and smiled, 'Lizzie, I do love it when you sit a while with me.'

Elizabeth smiled fondly back, and sat at the chair in the corner. Her prayer to God had always been that she would serve him no matter what. Even if this meant they would not have the nicest house or the smartest clothes. These were not to be things that she would think about. The rooms they were living in were simple, but Elizabeth did not mind. She had her husband and her calling from God to support George and to learn more and more about the Father she served. The shelves in the room were lined with books and the room had a slight smell of the fire that was burning in the grate. George's desk was covered in paper and his old, beloved Bible sat open in front of him. He swept back his hair off of his face and looked at his wife. She was as delightful as ever, he thought to himself, and nearly hopping with excitement about something.

More Love

'I will write some more to Anne and tell her how wonderful everything is. We are truly blessed by God, I feel like I might burst!'

'Indeed' George replied, 'I am happy every day, because every day has a little bit of Lizzie in them.' Elizabeth chuckled, 'Whatever do you mean?' she exclaimed.

'Well, my days are all the brighter because you are in them and the way that you are joyful and thankful, and as our dear old gentleman prayed, of a comfort to me.' Elizabeth's chuckle turned into an outright laugh. The dear old gentleman was a man in their congregation who had taken to regularly praying for George and Elizabeth that they might be of mutual comfort to one another. Elizabeth had found this a funny turn of phrase and they regularly joked together about it – but could see how this man's prayers were being answered every day.

She settled herself down again and took up her writing things. Elizabeth was content and thanked God regularly, remembering that all good things came from him, she rarely forgot him. Her life overflowed with blessings, and her heart too. A thankful heart and a kind spirit were something that Elizabeth tried to practice. It showed, her many friends loved her and learnt a lot from her about having faith in God. George and Elizabeth passed many an hour sat in quiet industry, George working on the things needed to support his church, Elizabeth writing to her friends and family and reading from scripture. Sometimes they both read to one another, or chatted about their family or the people whom they looked after as minister and wife. They giggled and joked together and had a great time, friends with one another, enjoying their time together. They were very happy. Elizabeth stood up and stretched her arms.

'I must get on with the baking I had planned,' she said 'Mrs H has been unwell and I am convinced that some of the gingerbread I make will do her the world of good. A little treat like that can only please her I think!' She grinned at George and made her way to the kitchen to begin baking. This was another thing that she enjoyed immensely. She loved caring for the house and for George and she was committed to being as useful and serving God in whatever small or large task she was presented with.

A few months later Elizabeth sat at the kitchen table with her writing things in front of her.

'Lizzie with a baby must sound quite funny to you' Elizabeth declared in her letter as she wrote to her friend Miss Thurston, 'I have to say it is in equal measure a delightful and challenging time.' Since she was a little girl Elizabeth loved babies and Elizabeth loved her little daughter that had just been born. However, having a baby and looking after it was really quite hard work and Elizabeth was tired and sometimes worried. Elizabeth laid her pen down and considered for a moment.

More Love

It was quite a change to become a mother, she felt. The girls that she had watched become mothers had a sudden seriousness to them that before she had not understood. Now, however, she knew that this strange, mysterious world that was motherhood was wondrous and difficult and joyful, all at the same time. She heard a noise. A loud sucking noise from Annie's thumb, the baby was awake and Elizabeth was needed! Supper! Elizabeth rose in a rush, tidied her letters into a pile and placed her pen upon them. It would have to do, not tidy enough, but small babies do not wait.

Elizabeth sat and combed Annie's hair. It would fall in a sweet curl if Elizabeth brushed it just right. She found herself loving her daughter more and more as she got used to being a mother. She scooped up the little girl in her arms and kissed her all over her face. The baby giggled. Such a lovely noise! Elizabeth went to the cabinet next to the crib and picked out some clothes for Annie. The ladies at church had made her so many lovely outfits that Elizabeth couldn't choose what to put on her girl.

'Come along, my little lamb. Time to get you dressed and ready for the service. You shall be baptised today, by your papa no less.' Elizabeth and George were determined to bring their daughter up in the ways of God.

Nearly two years later, while Annie toddled around at Elizabeth's feet a new baby, a boy, was swaddled

Elizabeth Prentiss

and cuddled on Elizabeth's lap. The little boy was called Eddy and Elizabeth was overjoyed with him. Unfortunately the baby cried a good deal. He would cry and cry and Elizabeth and George would pace up and down with him trying to calm him, singing hymns until they ran out of things to sing. Elizabeth would think to herself that she had memorised the entire hymnal through the night hours pacing with her grumpy baby.

'I am miserable, George,' Elizabeth said one day in a quiet voice. 'I miss my times when I sit and pray and read my Bible. I miss feeling the peace of God as I spend time with him. I spend all my hours with a cross and poorly baby and I have no time or energy for anything else. What am I to do?'

George took his wife's hand and held it tightly. The past months had been terribly difficult for his lovely Lizzie. She had gotten so thin that he worried for her health. He thought for a moment.

'You must remember, my Lizzie, that now is a time for action. The babies are small and your time is pressured, God does not expect you to pray and pray when your little ones need your attention. He is not like that! He will be pleased with the prayers and time that you can give him. He is still near, despite what it must feel like.'

Elizabeth listened, she knew this was true, but she still felt bereft of her devotional time, the time she spent before the children had been born when she

More Love

had all the time in the world to learn about God. She wondered how she would ever know the presence of God closely again.

Elizabeth opened the door to her home. It was a couple of years after Eddy had been born and she had spent a good time away with her friends and family and felt rested and ready to return and care for the children. The doctor's advice that she should recover from being so worn out was good advice and she was glad to have taken it. She dashed through the house, excited to see her little ones. Annie looked up as Elizabeth entered the room, 'Mamma!' She shouted and grabbed hold of her mother's skirts so tightly that Elizabeth thought she might topple on top of her girl. She swung her into her arms and held her so tightly that little Annie gasped for breath. 'My girl! I missed you! I'm so glad to see you!' The two stood there for a minute breathing in each other deeply, Annie's head buried in her mother's shoulder.

'Mamma, Eddy is making funny noises when he breathes.' Annie whispered in her mother's ear. Elizabeth tipped her head back and looked into Annie's face.

'What do you mean?' She was instantly worried, Eddy had always been a sick and poorly boy.

'Nurse says it is nothing to worry about, but he does sound very strange when he coughs and coughs.' Annie looked concerned. Elizabeth gently put her daughter down.

'Carry on with your reading, my darling, I'm going to check on your brother. No worries though, my sweetheart, God is good, he never makes a mistake!'

Elizabeth went up the stairs towards the nursery and opened the door. The nurse that had looked after the children was pacing up and down with little Eddy in her arms. Elizabeth walked over and looked at her boy. Immediately she knew that something was very wrong.

'Nurse! How long has he been so unwell?' She almost shouted but managed to stop herself from sounding so worried and cross. She took the child from the nurse and held him to her chest. Eddy was so light and although he was about the right size for his age he was a bit floppy and not at all strong. Eddy grasped at his mother and coughed again. The nurse wrung her hands.

'Oh, I don't know what to do,' she cried, 'none of the remedies I have tried make it any better, it's only a cough, but it just won't go away!'

Elizabeth uttered a silent prayer that her boy would be well. She knew that this was not just a cough.

Elizabeth sat at her desk writing in her journal. 'Thank you Father,' she wrote, 'thank you that my boy is still alive. I know that I don't have him for much longer. It is worth a good deal to see his face though, it is so brimful of life and sunshine and gladness.'

Although Elizabeth suspected that Eddy would not live for very long she still thanked God for him.

More Love

He was a lovely boy and both Elizabeth and George delighted in him.

It was the summer of 1851, Annie was sitting where her mother often sat, at the writing desk. The family had moved to New York where George had accepted a job working for a church as the pastor .

'Mamma, I shall write to Papa, and tell him that we miss him dreadfully whilst he is away in Maine visiting with his friend.'

'Of course, Annie, he will enjoy hearing from you. Make sure you write some happiness into your letter too, not just grumbling about missing him.' Elizabeth smiled fondly at her daughter, so similar to herself. Elizabeth always missed George whilst he was away and this time was no exception. Annie had been unwell and had had several nose bleeds which had panicked the little girl and caused Elizabeth to be concerned. However, there were happy things to think of too, one of which was trying to climb up her skirt!

'Ow!' Elizabeth cried as she tried to prise the tiny kitten, one of two, that the children were now proud owners of. 'Annie Louise, your kitten is tearing your mother to shreds!'

'Mamma, that is not my one, that is Eddy's kitten. Surely you can see the patch above his nose?' Annie looked across at her mother with a stern expression upon her face. Elizabeth looked at the little ball of fluff

Elizabeth Prentiss

and claws and noticed that there was indeed a patch upon its face. Eddy appeared in the room.

'My catty!' he cried and scooped up the kitten gratefully off of Elizabeth's lap. He nuzzled the kitten to his face. Elizabeth was glad to see her son so happy and thanked the Lord once again for keeping him alive until now. However, sadly it was not to last.

The weather was cold by the time December came. The rooms were hard to keep heated and Christmas came and went in a blur of illness and concern. Elizabeth was expecting another baby and that was a strain for her also. Eddy was increasingly poorly and Elizabeth spent hours of anxiety trying to help him feel better.

'I don't want to die,' Eddy said to his mother, after another night of no sleep and fever.

'*Why?*' replied his mother, '*You know it is a great deal pleasanter in heaven than it is here. Little boys don't have the headache there. I should love dearly to go if God said I might.*'

'Yes,' interjected Annie. 'Don't you know how we used to sing about the happy land?' But Annie could not keep on, she stifled a sob and left the room, all too aware of what lay ahead and unable to say anything to make it better.

Eddy was ordered to take a warm bath by the doctor. Elizabeth knew that this was not going to be sufficient to ease her boy's suffering. However, as he got out and was wrapped up in his night clothes to return to bed, he said;

More Love

'Tell me a story, Mamma?' Elizabeth leant next to his bed and began to rock it gently.

'What do you wish to hear about, my love?'

'A little boy,' answered Eddy.

'Ah, of course.' Elizabeth hummed to herself a minute whilst she thought and then began, '*Mamma knows a dear little boy who was very sick. His head ached and he felt sick all over. God said, I must let that little lamb come into my fold; then his head will never ache again, and he will be a very happy little lamb. Would you like to know the name of this little boy?*' Elizabeth wiped a stray tear that was running down her face.

'Yes, yes Mamma!' Eddy cried eagerly.

'It was Eddy.' She took his hand and kissed it gently.

Elizabeth sat down once again at her writing desk. It was Friday. She had told her son that lovely story on the Sunday before. Throughout that week he had not slept at all well or been able to be comfortable for very long. However, he had not seemed to be in much pain. Elizabeth wiped at more tears that were falling on her cheeks. She wrote:

Eddy's loving and gentle spirit ascended to that world where thousands of holy children and the blessed company of angels and our blessed Lord Jesus, I doubt not, joyfully welcomed him. Now we are able to say, 'It is well with the child!' Elizabeth paused, and then continued, '*Oh' said the gardener, as he passed down the garden-walk, 'who plucked that flower? His fellow-servants answered, 'The Master!' And the gardener held his peace.*

Elizabeth Prentiss

It came time for the next baby to be born. Elizabeth was not particularly well when Bessie was born, she had not recovered from losing Eddy. She caught a common illness after the birth and was confined to her bedroom.

'Oh!' Elizabeth muttered to herself crossly. 'Oh, I must get up, I can hear the baby.'

George entered the room. He looked at his wife.

'You indeed must not get up. Stay there. You are far too ill to leave your bed. Nurse will take care of Bessie. Stay in your bed until I get back.' George sounded stern, but he was ever so worried again for the health of his wife.

'My baby is only a month old! I want to look after her!' Elizabeth wept frustrated tears into her pillow.

'I will get the nurse to bring her to you, my love. Then you may hold her and love her.' George left to fetch the child and her nurse.

Elizabeth waited patiently. She heard them coming and sat herself up. They entered the room and placed baby Bessie in her arms. Elizabeth gasped. She was overwhelmed by a strong sense that Bessie too would not stay long but that God was calling her home. Elizabeth was convinced that the baby was seriously ill.

Bessie was returned to her room and Elizabeth reminded to stay in hers to recover. She could hear the pitiful cries of the baby.

'No! I will not stay here,' Elizabeth gasped to herself. She slipped out of bed. She was too ill to stand. She crawled on her hands and knees towards the

More Love

nursery and Bessie. She reached the room and could hear the cries of the baby. George came in too.

'Elizabeth!' he cried, 'you are too ill! You must return to your bed!'

He carried her back to her room and firmly placed her back in her sick bed. Elizabeth continued to hear the cries of her baby and weep into her pillow. Eventually she crawled again into the baby's room. The child was terribly ill. She grabbed her out of the nurse's arms and sat on the floor cradling her baby. George thumped up the stairs, returning from his trip out. He entered the room and his faced paled. He now could see how ill Bessie was. He took her into his arms and baptised her then and there.

God help me, my baby, my baby! Elizabeth wrote, another child had died. God never makes a mistake was Elizabeth's repeated thought through those terrible days. She wrote:
One child and two green graves are mine
This is God's gift to me;
A bleeding, fainting, broken heart —
This is my gift to Thee.

Writing, Writing, Writing

Elizabeth sat with Annie on her lap. The poor child was only young, just six years old, and the second funeral of a sibling had affected her deeply. The child would not play, she just sat with her head buried in her mother's chest.

'Annie, my darling, don't you wish to play or get up and go about somewhere?'

'I don't.'

'It would be good for you if you would consider it? Sitting about all day without anything to do is not good for a child. What can I get for you to do? What would you like?'

'Nothing, Mother.' Annie mumbled, not raising her head. Elizabeth bent down her own head, her hair was not as proper as it normally was – grief reduced Elizabeth's efforts at such things – strands fell out from her hastily tied bun and brushed onto Annie's head.

'That tickles!' Annie wriggled and sat up a bit, fumbling at her head as if there were feathers all over it.

More Love

'Ah, tickling, is that what I can interest you in?' Elizabeth pushed a smile onto her face, she wasn't at all interested in tickling herself. She would have happily returned to her bed and stayed there.

'I think that I shouldn't be interested in anything.' Annie's face fell from momentary happiness back to grim and miserable reality. Remembering every minute that she was two siblings short of a complete family.

'Why? What makes you think that?' Elizabeth gently turned her daughter's face towards her, noting the dark bags under her eyes and the red rims from crying and rubbing them.

'I miss my brother and sister so much.' She sobbed and cried and threw her arms around her neck. They sat there for a moment. 'Where are they, Mother? How can they be there one moment and gone the next? How can this be? How can you be alive one moment and not there anymore the next? I cannot stop thinking about their tiny coffins. What has happened to my brother and sister?!' She fairly wailed at this and the huge, breathless sobs that engulfed her shook her and her mother's bodies. Elizabeth held onto her tightly, rocking her back and forwards and resting her head onto her daughter's hair. She breathed in the familiar Annie scent. They sat for a minute. They were the very picture of unhappiness and unity. Could such a thing be? They were together in their sadness. Elizabeth breathed deeply and raised her head back up again. She loved her daughter so much and hated that this was what she had to suffer.

Elizabeth Prentiss

'Your Eddy and Bessie are in heaven. I know this to be true. They have gone straight there. They are in the arms of the Lord, just like you are in my arms.'

'I wish they were here, you could hold them instead.' These words tore away at Elizabeth, how could this be endured? She wished that too, but she had also learnt something in her suffering, something that she could share with her daughter.

'Eddy and Bessie are better off than we are. They are no longer in pain, not the kind of pain we feel in our bodies or the kind of pain that we feel in our mind. They are happy, truly and completely happy. It is us indeed that are too sad for words.' Elizabeth straightened her back and leaned backwards to fully look into her daughter's dear and wonderful face. 'But, darling child, we can learn from this too. God draws us closer to him. To whom else can we go when the pain in our hearts is so bad? Can Father help us?' Annie paused to consider this, her father was magnificent and loving, but even at the tender age of six Annie could see that he could not help her as his grief was a big wound upon his own life that he could not heal, nor heal hers.

'He loves me, but I don't think he can make me happier. He is too sad.'

'Indeed, Father's heart is as broken as mine and yours. He cannot make you happy. He cannot change how we feel. But God our Father can. He will not bring your brother and sister back, and we should not want it, for they are better now than they ever

More Love

were here. Yet, we can learn to draw closer to God in our sadness.'

'I don't know how to do that,' Annie said honestly.

'Nor do I, if I think about it as something that I must get up and *do*. It is not like that. We must say to God that we are ready to be nearer him. We give our lives over to him and say that he is in charge.'

'Maybe I can do that.' Annie wasn't really sure, Elizabeth could tell from her face. She was so young to learn this lesson, one that some adults would never understand. Elizabeth barely could manage it herself, but she knew that it was the only way. This was her role as a mother, to keep on telling God's ways to her daughter, to prepare her for a life lived for God. Maybe she wouldn't understand it all right now, but eventually, perhaps, she would. Elizabeth's wish was that Annie would go further, do better, know more wisely than she had ever done. Was that not every parent's wish, that their children would go beyond what they ever could?

Eventually Annie had felt she wished to go for a walk. Elizabeth had determined that they both should do it, for their health if nothing else. So they had put on their coats and shoes and strode out into the fresh air. The normal things of life had continued, birds were singing their songs, the odd butterfly presented itself for their inspection and tentative delight. The world God had made still turned, and this was reassuring. They had walked far enough to tire themselves out and had eaten their supper together, not waiting for George to return from his duties, as Elizabeth had wanted to immerse herself in loving her daughter, not leaving her to own devices even to eat a meal alone. This was for Elizabeth's benefit as much as Annie's. It had been possible to draw a bath that night, for bath nights were a rare treat, not something to be squandered. Tired bodies deserved a warm bath and extra attention and Annie's pale frame had indeed improved with a warm bath and a nightie heated by the stove in the kitchen. Tucked into bed Elizabeth had told her stories made up by herself for at least an hour. The child asked questions and added ideas of her own until she was too sleepy to do anything but listen. Eventually her listening happened with her eyes closed and Elizabeth bent down to rest her ear on the gently rising and falling chest. Asleep. Peacefully. This was the beginning of helping her daughter heal. Not what about herself?

Elizabeth's own healing would not be quite so simple. Unfortunately grown-ups never are simple creatures and Elizabeth was prone to thinking very hard about things. Eventually she stumbled upon a way in which she could start to think about the deaths of two of her children. She wrote poetry. These poems were prayers. They were a way to talk to God using ideas and pictures and thoughts to express something that was deep in her heart. Prayer need not be simply out loud, requests and thanks and apologies. No, Elizabeth's poems poured from her straight to God's ears. It was different, but it was good.

More Love

Elizabeth stood alone in her kitchen. The lady that came in to help her sometimes had not been there for a month. Nobody had been there for a month. Nobody except the doctor. How could so much have changed? Elizabeth's thoughts turned backwards as she remembered her glorious summer holiday. It had been so much needed after the dark miserable months they had endured. Annie had come to life, it felt, hopping and skipping through fields and farms with other children who had gone with them from the church. Then they had attended the great Crystal Palace Exhibition and it had amazed them. Finally, the fun had continued with her young cousin Louisa [1] visiting. Louisa was alive with energy and good spirits. Annie had spent a lot of time with her laughing and dancing and enjoying someone who felt like an older sister. Elizabeth had delighted in watching their high jinx and capers. But, as if from nowhere, tragedy once more returned to Elizabeth's house.

'Oh, Elizabeth, I do feel unwell. Gosh, I can barely lift up my legs.' Louisa tried to sit up in her bed, Elizabeth firmly pressed her back down again.

'Do not sit up, the doctor has told you that you are to rest.' Elizabeth walked around the side of the bed and reached for a small glass container.

'I am very glad that I have no appetite for food, otherwise being told all I could eat was arrowroot

---

[1]. This was not the same Louisa as Elizabeth had taught with in Richmond, or her sister.

would cause me to despair.' Louisa bravely smiled but really she was too ill to manage it. Elizabeth poured a spoon of the mixture and held it for Louisa to take.

'Do you think you can try to sleep, my dear? Shall I leave you for an hour or so, then I will come back and check on that horrible rash you have?' Louisa closed her eyes and nodded. Sleep had not been easy for her and Elizabeth was extremely concerned about the rash that Louisa had developed. It did not look quite right, but it was not like anything that Elizabeth had seen before. However, the doctor had not been terribly worried. Louisa had even started to feel a bit better than she had at first. The vomiting had stopped, at least. Yet it was not to last. Later that day the fever returned with a vengeance. The doctor was downstairs speaking with George's mother when Elizabeth cried out,

'Oh, come quickly, do hurry!'

However, it was too late and suddenly, Louisa was gone. It had been malignant smallpox, an unusual kind that did not look like the usual ravages of smallpox. They had missed it. The doctor was insistent,

'You must all be vaccinated, the house must be completely scrubbed. This is very serious, you must act quickly.' Elizabeth flew about trying to rush away the disease with cleaning and haste. It was not to be. Annie became ill and it seemed as if all of Elizabeth's deepest, darkest, most horrifying fears were about to happen.

Quarantine was imposed upon the house. Nobody was allowed to visit, and the occupants could not leave. Elizabeth nursed Annie around the clock, barely sleeping or resting, all the while begging with God that he spare her daughter.

Elizabeth continued to stand, alone, in the kitchen. The walls appeared to her as if they had moved two feet inwards, she felt that she might never leave, speak to another human again. Her thoughts were hard to control, with nothing distracting her from them. She sat at the scrubbed kitchen table and wrote to her mother-in-law.

'I am afraid that these awful diseases lurk all around our house, ready to take their next victim. Are my children all to be grasped by them? Annie is so precious, so dear to me, I write to beg of your prayers for her. Ultimately though, I know I must give her to God and let him do his will.'

Annie was to recover, it was very close though.

It began to become clear that poems were not the only form of writing that Elizabeth should undertake in that bleak time of sadness. As it turned out, writing was something of a mission for her.

Elizabeth, George, Annie and Elizabeth's brother all sat in front of the fire in the Prentiss' house. The warmth from the fire pervaded the room and with a blanket upon her lap Elizabeth was quite comfortable.

'Well, my dear sister, your pen has never been still, not since you were a child.' Elizabeth's brother, commented.

'That is true! I think that if I can write for children about Jesus and his love. If I can show them about him then they might love him as children and continue to do so for all their days. Even during times when I am unwell, this is something I can do to serve God.' Elizabeth was shy all of a sudden, explaining her desire that was burning in her heart. 'If I can help just one child know that there is a father in heaven who loves them, I will have had a great privilege.'

'Elizabeth, our own children are testimony to that, you will help more than just one child, I am certain. These "Little Suzy" stories will bless more than just a few children. They will bless many.' George looked at his wife with adoration.

'Come along then,' cried Annie, 'I want to hear the rest, you adults must stop talking so Mother can keep reading her book!' The adults chuckled, this was a bit rude, but they shared the child's desire, and promptly were silent for the book reading to continue.

Letters and Holidays

The postman knocked upon the door. Elizabeth fairly flew towards it, throwing her dust cloth down to the floor with enthusiasm. She flung open the front door, the postman stepped back in surprise.

'Well, you are prompt! Here are another handful. One of them has a postmark all the way from the south on it!' The postman smiled at Elizabeth. Elizabeth swept stray hairs away from her forehead and eagerly reached out to grab the bundle of letters, some addressed in the fine handwriting of mothers, others in childish scrawl.

'Oh, thank you! What a delight!' Elizabeth restrained herself from hugging the poor bewildered postman and shut the door with restraint behind his retreating figure. She stamped, somewhat petulantly, on the abandoned dust cloth as she went to sit in her favourite chair to read the letters.

'Oh, bliss!' she commented. The letters were all from children and families commenting on what a difference her writing had made to them. This was a

More Love

great deal better than housework. Housework was dull. Dull and repetitive. As soon as it was done it needed doing again. And again! Elizabeth found this very boring. She was tempted to give in to this boredom and complain bitterly. However, as with other trials in her life, she decided to see the good in it.

'I shall find what the Lord will teach me from housework!' she declared to the empty, and still dusty, room. 'Lord, school me with patience and grace for the boring work that a woman has to do to run a house. I'm ready,' Elizabeth said, expectantly, as if the lesson she desired was going to appear before her immediately. The answer was to come later, in a deeper understanding of finding God in the small, mundane chores that life always demands. The things that are never finished, but that help us to focus our minds on God. Elizabeth would later talk about them as 'Christ's school' that taught her humility and grace.

The summer of 1854 blazed through the windows of the house. The heat was sometimes unbearable. Elizabeth was glad she was no longer pregnant, being pregnant in this heat was definitely too much to tolerate! George was sitting opposite his wife, watching as the new baby nursed.

'I am glad my little girl has a healthy appetite!' he commented.

'Indeed, perhaps she takes after her father?' Elizabeth suggested.

Elizabeth Prentiss

'Well, if so, Minnie is indeed a blessed child!' George chuckled, then coughed. He stretched out in his chair. He was infinitely tired these days.

'Are you alright, George?' Elizabeth frowned with concern.

'Yes, I'm fine. Just a little tired. Nothing compared to you, I expect.' Elizabeth was up all night with her baby. 'Annie is so, so happy with her new sister, isn't she?' he said, changing the subject. Elizabeth noticed, but didn't press him.

'Yes, she is. Yesterday she mentioned Eddy and Bessie, I think they are on her mind. She is worried, I believe.'

'Yes, well, you are too, are you not?' George asked.

'Yes, of course, Minnie is so small, she reminds me of Eddy. I fear that her composition is not dissimilar.' Elizabeth had noticed the similarities in the two children and feared that the baby would be sickly, just like her older brother had been. 'But they are only lent to us from God, they are not ours to keep. We must look after them and teach them God's ways but they are not ours forever.'

'We must entrust her to the Lord, just like with the others, his will is best and good.' George hoped that the Lord's will was the same as his, or was that the other way around?

A knock came at the front door. Annie sat bolt upright.

More Love

'Is that her?' she asked.

'I expect so,' said her mother, getting up. Elizabeth had received a letter a few days before from a lady across town telling her about a little girl she knew of who was extremely poor. Elizabeth had decided to try and help.

'Hello,' Elizabeth said to the tiny waif of a girl standing on her doorstep. 'Do come in, I'm pleased to meet you, my name is Elizabeth.' The girl smiled shyly.

'I am Jane, Miss,' she said. 'Thank you for inviting me.'

'Don't call me 'Miss', I am Elizabeth, you have beautiful manners though. You must tell your mother I said so.' Elizabeth ushered the girl into the kitchen where Annie was waiting. Annie leapt up and surrounded the girl in a huge hug. Startled, Jane stood there for a moment. Then, coming to her senses, she returned the embrace, the small smile reappearing.

'Well, this is my daughter Annie, she has been excited to meet you too. We've made you some breakfast, would you like to have some?' The little girl's eyes moved to the pile of food on the table that Annie had been collecting all morning. She looked amazed, and really hungry.

'Oh, yes please!' Sitting down she began to eat, fast. Then, remembering herself she slowed down and looked all around her. 'You have a beautiful house. I like all the flowers.' Elizabeth loved to decorate her house with things that she found outside, she had quite a talent for it.

'Thank you. You're kind. Is the breakfast good?'

'Oh yes, it is wonderful!'

'Is your mother feeling better?' Elizabeth was aware that Jane's mother was unwell and that her father was struggling to keep the family looked after, to earn enough money and to keep things going well at home.

'She ails sometimes, then feels better. The doctor hasn't been in a while 'cause Father says we can't afford it.' Elizabeth resolved to send him round on her say so, and pay the bill.

'I will look after your mother. You must not worry.' She reached down to a basket at her feet. 'I have some clothes and things here that may be of use to you, and a few things that were sent to me for you, stockings and such, that I think won't fit you (although they were intended for you) but may fit your baby sister. What do you think? Should you like them?'

'Yes, please. Mother said to say 'thank you' for all your kindness.'

'Tell your mother it is nothing, that God says we must look after those who are in need. This is how we are trying to do it, isn't it Annie?' Annie nodded vigorously. 'We can't help everyone in New York, but we can definitely try and help you!'

'That's right, Mother, what is it you said about raindrops?' Annie screwed up her face in concentration. Elizabeth looked at her bewildered.

'Raindrops? Oh, yes, I remember, that each time we help someone it feels like it is only a drop in a bucket

More Love

of all the people who need help, but, *yet somebody must look out for the drops.*' Elizabeth knew that God cared for every last person, just like the Bible said he knew about even the little sparrows, and that her duty was to care too. Not just to fix the entire problem but remember the individuals, and look after them.

Elizabeth looked up from the paper that was perched on her lap. Her writing was going so well these days, a new book was to be published soon, called 'Henry and Bessie, or what they did in the country' and she so enjoyed filling some of her time with penning these lovely stories. However, it was hard to concentrate with all the current distractions! Annie shrieked a distance away from her and Elizabeth resignedly put her pen down. The sun was blazing down on her face and the sound of the waves crashing onto the beach touched her ears. They had come for a long holiday at Ocean House at Cape Elizabeth. Six weeks of sun and rocky beaches for climbing and scrambling along. Elizabeth could see Annie from where she was sitting, perched on a flattish stone. Annie was bent over at her middle, with her bottom quite stuck in the air, carefully examining the contents of a recently exposed rock pool. Every now and again she would poke at something therein with a stick that she held in her hand and peer even closer at the reaction.

Just at that moment George flopped down next to Elizabeth on a rocky outcrop . He looked just like a boy, trousers rolled up to his knees, glistening legs

Elizabeth Prentiss

wet from salty sea water, a handkerchief tied around his head and a fishing net cast down by his feet with the relish of successful rock pooling.

'You, my dear, look as if you are quite a thirteen-year-old. How goes crabbing today?' Elizabeth grinned at her husband.

'Well,' he said with triumph, 'as you ask – I have cast my net only a few times and the crabs fairly walked into it. I have obviously missed my vocation as a fisherman!'

'Ah, I believe not, you are a fisher of men, just as Christ called us all to be,' Elizabeth said.

'It is true, I am that. I am a fisher of men who is glad of this holiday. I was greatly in need of a rest, and so were you. Your health seems much improved, and that of the children.' At this George looked at their youngest child, Minnie, who was sat upon a blanket just in front of them. She was putting stones in little piles as she could reach them from around her, and then knocking down her towers that she had made.

'Quite the knight of the realm, our girl there,' George smiled at her, 'she knocks over those towers with the aplomb of a British soldier at arms!'

'Indeed, she gives them no quarter!' Elizabeth joked. She sighed contentedly and turned her face further towards the sun. This was doing them all good.

'We must remember to rest more,' George commented.

'Yes, the Lord ordained a day of rest every seven at the beginning of all creation, he did it knowing that

More Love

we are creatures that need it. We must make sure that we follow his commands and do not push ourselves to work more than we should.'

'The demands of the congregation are hard to juggle though, I find. What am I to do when called upon to visit the sick and dying, or to help a man who needs it? Tell them it is my day off?' George huffed out a frustrated sigh.

'I know, I do not pretend to have the answer. We must seek the Lord for his guidance, however else can any of us succeed in any endeavour. One thing I do know, we must rest more, however we come about to achieve it.' Elizabeth was firm, rest was important, it was ordained by God and she was to help her family, her worn out husband, to seek after the ways of God – and that included taking breaks!

'It feels as if we have hardly been away.' Elizabeth grumbled. It was the following January and the summer holiday they had was a distant dream. Life back home had become difficult again.

'We must persevere. We must also enjoy our time out!' George took his wife's arm in the crook of his and strolled on towards their destination. They were visiting friends of theirs in the evening whilst the children slept at home with the nurse. Suddenly they could hear footsteps behind them, running. Elizabeth swung about. It was the cook from the house next door.

Elizabeth Prentiss

'Oh, Miss!' she cried, bending over to catch her breath and speaking through gasps, 'Oh, Miss, do hurry, it is the baby, she is ever so ill, you must come quickly!' Elizabeth felt as if her arms and legs had gone numb. She truly understood the term 'frozen in panic' at that moment. George grabbed her by the hand and tugged her into a run. Elizabeth came to and fled to her house as fast as she could possibly make her legs go. All thoughts of anything left her mind, all there was in it was panic. They both crashed up the path to their house, swung open the front door and ascended the stairs as quickly as they could. Upon arrival in the nursery room they saw the doctor bent over Minnie's bed. She was quite still. Hearing them arrive the doctor straightened his back and turned around. His face was very grave.

'She is unconscious, I'm afraid,' he said sombrely.

'How can this be?' Elizabeth was shrieking now. 'She was well earlier today, perhaps she began to suffer from a slight cough, but nothing that would expect this!' George put his arm around his wife's shoulders, Elizabeth noticed, at the edge of her consciousness that he was trembling.

'It has descended upon her very quickly. It is bad. You must prepare yourselves.' The doctor did not need to tell them what they must prepare themselves for, the dread returned to them with familiarity. Their daughter was dying.

'Oh, my girl!' Elizabeth sobbed and ran to the bedside, she crouched down and grasped the small

More Love

hand in her own. It was too tiny, too fragile. This child was Elizabeth's own, part of her own body. Surely she could not lose another one?

George and Elizabeth sat either side of Minnie's bedside for that entire night. The cough had developed into breathing difficulties and the child's face had lost its healthy childish pinkness and had taken on a deathly purple hue as each breath was fought for and hard won. Flying through Elizabeth's mind was every happy memory that she had had with this beautiful girl. She was so exhausted that she could not even lift her thoughts to prayer. She knew that this child was God's and that it was to him that her life was turned, whether in life or death. She must be ready to see her go to the Lord if that was his will. Should what she gives the Lord in her life be of little value, a token here or there, an amount of money to the church or some of her plentiful time? No! It should be her utmost treasure, the thing that she values the most, that should be her gift to the Lord. Her sacrifice. She must be ready to let her daughter go, if that is what is required of her.

However, despite many nights and days of illness, the Lord did not take Minnie home. She survived, but it was to be many more months before she was recovered. During that time Elizabeth wrote another book that was published, called 'Little Susy's Six Teachers'. That summer Elizabeth and the girls went off on holiday to a farm. It was to be a very happy time for them.

'Mother, look! I have found the biggest one yet!' cried Annie holding aloft a large, white strawberry.

'It's not ripe, my darling! Don't pick them until they are ruby red, it will not taste good until then.' Elizabeth chuckled to herself, what joy there was in strawberry picking. Up and down the rows they went, stooped low and picking and plopping into baskets. Minnie, Elizabeth noted, was not doing the plopping into baskets, just the picking and then the eating!

'Mother, look at Minnie's face, it is entirely red with juice!' Annie was indignant, that was not why they were here! They were not here to eat them, that was later! Minnie turned around to her mother and grinned. Elizabeth delighted in her, and her happy face, red with strawberry juice was a vast improvement to purple with illness.

'Now, Minnie,' she said, without any crossness at all, 'pick the red strawberries and put them in the pot here. So we can eat them later, back at the farm.' Minnie nodded and went toddling off grabbing all kinds and qualities of strawberries and putting them in the little pot that she carried with her. She could be heard singing to herself:

'Put it in the pop, put it in the pop, put it in the pop!'

'Pot!' shouted Annie, two rows over, 'it is pot! Not 'pop'!'

More Love

'Don't be too harsh with her, Annie, she is just learning. At least she isn't eating them all anymore!' Although looking at the 'pop' full of misshapen and squashed strawberries she wasn't sure if anyone would be eating Minnie's contribution to the strawberry harvest! Elizabeth strolled contentedly over to the side of the field where there stood a bench. She reached into the pocket of her apron and pulled out the stub of pencil and the notebook that were buried within. She sat down on the bench and wrote the final lines of a hymn that had been swimming around in her head.

More love to Thee, oh Christ, more love to Thee!
Hear Thou the prayer I make on bended knee.
This is my earnest plea
More love, oh Christ, to Thee
More love to Thee, more love to Thee!

Once earthly joy I craved, sought peace and rest
Now Thee alone I seek, give what is best.
This all my prayer shall be
More love, oh Christ to Thee
More love to Thee, more love to Thee!

Let sorrow do its work, send grief or pain;
Sweet are Thy messengers, sweet their refrain,
When they can sing with me,
More love, O Christ, to Thee,
More love to Thee, more love to Thee!

Elizabeth Prentiss

*Then shall my latest breath whisper Thy praise
This be the parting cry my heart shall raise
Still all my prayer shall be
More love, oh Christ to Thee
More love to Thee, more love to Thee!*

This was to become a hymn that Elizabeth was famous for. It is still known today. Born out of all the sufferings that Elizabeth had endured and a faithful devotion to God and knowing him better, the hymn was Elizabeth's attempt to cry out to God during the hard times, not in despair but in rejoicing.

However, it was difficult to hold onto this and during the next few months Elizabeth's resolve to endure sufferings for the benefit of knowing Christ was sorely tested. She became ill, so ill that she was close to death. She welcomed the thought of it.

She wrote in her journal:

Now contrary to my hopes and expectations, I find myself almost well again. At first, having got my heart set toward heaven and after fancying myself almost there, I felt disappointed to find its gates still shut against me. But God was very good to me and taught me to yield in this point to his wiser and better will; he made me, as far as I know, as peaceful in the prospect of living as joyful in the prospect of dying.

Elizabeth went on to recover, and to have another baby. This time a boy, called George. 'I shall call you

More Love

little George for now or simply baby, and then when you're older 'Young George' shall be your name. Otherwise no one shall know if it's you or your father we're calling for!' Elizabeth whispered into her young boy's ear, kissing him at the same time.

'I am quite well,' Elizabeth's husband insisted, lying in his bed, hot with fever, yet again.

'I hardly think you are,' said Elizabeth stoutly. She could be cross and this was one of those times.

'I must try to get up, there is much to do.' George went to sit up. Elizabeth pushed him back into his pillows.

'All you are fit for, if you try to get up, is falling back over again. Stay there!' At that moment the door sounded and the entrance of the doctor and one of the church leaders could be heard. Much discussion downstairs could be detected, although it was impossible to make out the content of it. Footsteps outside the room announced the arrival of said doctor and churchman.

'Come in, my friends, come in.' George sat himself up a little, under the stern eye of Elizabeth. The two men entered the room. The doctor spoke first.

'George, we have spent a good deal of time together recently, you having been so ill. Your latest bout of illness has laid you up for a long time. You are repeatedly unwell and overworked. I've come because I need to say to you …' George sat up straighter and interrupted.

Elizabeth Prentiss

'Good man, do not say it! I have so much work that must be done. God's work. I have parishioners to visit, ill folk who need their pastor, lectures, sermons, funerals, tea invites. All of this must be done.' Elizabeth sat down in despair, this was too much work for any man, never mind one who had such grief and illness inflicted upon him in his life. The doctor held up his hand.

'Now George, you must hear it. You are too ill. You must stop work, I am afraid I must insist upon it, for your health.' George sat back in his pillows with a sigh, he was defeated.

'But this is the task God has called me to,' he tried one more time.

'God has not called you to work yourself into an early grave,' the doctor said wisely.

'Think George what you said to me when we were at Cape Elizabeth. We must learn to take the Lord's rest when it comes. You have had to bear so much, I have failed you, I think; you have had to support your family through so many illnesses and sadnesses. It is more than anyone can sustain.' Elizabeth felt tears rolling down her cheeks as she spoke, so heavy was the guilt for her husband and his tired worn out body upon her. George looked upon her with compassion. It was then that the other man in the room began to speak.

'George, myself and the other elders at Mercer Street have been talking. We wish to see you well. You must rest. We have decided that we would like to

More Love

send you, and the rest of your family to Switzerland. To take the air, to recover. If and when you are better, we will welcome you back with shouts of joy! But you must get better. This is our gift to you for all yours and Elizabeth's hard work for us.' Elizabeth gasped. George looked amazed. Switzerland? This would be a great cure for George, the clear mountain air had done many a weary worker much good. Elizabeth was too stunned to speak and George looked to be flailing about for something to say.

'Excellent,' said the doctor, 'exactly what this doctor orders.'

Life in Switzerland

Elizabeth perched on the edge of her trunk, looking out as the great big steamer ship ploughed through the choppy ocean and away from the shore. The salty wind was fresh over her face and Elizabeth gasped as the odd blustery challenge of wind would win against her trying to take a breath. It swept in and blew the air fairly out of her mouth. She considered the position the family found itself in. Married for a long while now, George and she had suffered many trials and troubles and Elizabeth worried that all of this had brought George too low in health to recover. Having worked hard in his job in New York his health had suffered from his dedication to his calling. The church in New York were concerned and had decided to send the Prentiss family abroad, a common thing to do for the benefit of health. The year was 1858 and they were about to set off on another adventure.

'What troubles you, Mrs Prentiss?' Isabella, their beloved housemaid appeared at Elizabeth's side, a worried expression upon her face.

More Love

'Ah, Isabella, I am just thinking. I am worried for Mr Prentiss, and for his health.'

'The clear Swiss air should help that,' Isabella said encouragingly, she paused, 'and, you have so many gifts and treats sent with you from the church that his health may improve from putting on more weight!'

'Isabella, you are mischievous, but you are right! The church were so generous, not only to send us on this trip but to give us so many great gifts. I must, of course, make sure Annie does not eat her way through them before we arrive. Two weeks on a boat is a long time! We must make sure she spots plenty of sea birds and ships and other sights, to keep her entertained.'

'Of course, running around after little brother and sister will be exercise enough.' Isabella looked mildly concerned as she spoke, 'they are going to be a mischief themselves, let loose on a great ship like this!'

'Goodness, what have we let ourselves in for?' Elizabeth chuckled.

As it was they had let themselves in for two grey and foggy weeks on the ship that were rather colder than they had hoped. The brisk sea air, that had initially been so refreshing continued to cool into more of an arctic breeze. They were extremely glad to see land when they arrived at Normandy. From Normandy they went to Paris and met with friends, from Paris they journeyed to Switzerland.

'Look, Mama, look – beds on shelves!' Annie shouted as she looked down the sleeper train.

'Oh yes, my dear, I see what you mean, those will be our beds for the next few days.' Elizabeth regarded them closely, will they do? She wondered.

'Oh, however will we sleep on a train?' Annie squeaked, 'it is so exciting!'

'Miss Annie, you will be too tired to do anything else,' Isabella declared, unloading her bag and setting out her books of French that she had brought with her to learn from.

'Isabella, you are wonderful, you set such a good example to the children, studying the language of the place we are going to. Who could ask for a better helper than you?!' Elizabeth delighted, Isabella was much more than a maid, she was her friend and companion on this adventure.

'Ah, Mrs Prentiss, I am so glad you think so. I am learning, slowly.'

'Learning always feels a bit slow, when you get started, you are doing marvellously, just marvellously.'

'Indeed, I agree wholeheartedly!' George was putting down cases and handing others to the station master to put in the luggage carriage. He smiled at the children and Isabella. 'Now, who wants to see the dining car?'

'Oh, me! Me!' Annie squeaked again.

'Honestly, I do believe that child is getting more and more high pitched the higher up the mountains we travel,' declared George.

More Love

'How can you eat on a train? Where does the food come from? Will it all fall on the floor...?' Annie disappeared with her father, asking questions all the while. Elizabeth scooped up the baby, who had managed to crawl onto a bed and fall asleep and took themselves all off to find somewhere to sit.

As the train pulled into their final station the Prentiss family were glad to stop. They arrived in Geneva and were taken on a carriage, pulled by five black horses to their home up in the mountains. They were met by their friend, Mrs Buck.

'Oh, my dear friends, you must be tired from all your travelling. Do sit down, do rest, have some tea. We will get in your cases. Your other things arrived yesterday.' Mrs Buck clucked and fussed around them, weary as they were from walking the last little bit of their journey as the carriage wouldn't fit.

'We are weary but delighted, the air is already seeping into our bones, Mrs Buck,' George said as he lent to give their friend a kiss.

'Yes, and what a sweet little path that we walked up, winding around, giving us glimpses here and there of the mountains and the view, and the stream that sang to us as we walked next to it. The water was so clear and bubbly, I felt that I could not have believed such a perfect one existed if I had not seen it!' Elizabeth was gushing, she was so enamoured with her surroundings. 'All my life I have heard about these wonderful mountains, I knew of them from being a child, but I could never have believed they were this wonderful. Never.'

'Indeed, Elizabeth, they are more than any of us could quite believe. We felt like we had walked into a brilliant painting when we first arrived.' Mrs Buck said and she reached forwards and grasped Elizabeth's hand. She pressed it to her heart. 'You are here to rest and to get well, all of you, I pray that you will be better and better as each day passes. Now, we must show you your new home. It is small, but simply beautiful.'

The group turned a corner and there stood a perfect Swiss chalet. Just like in any picture that anyone had ever seen. It was made from logs of dark wood and had a big roof, almost like an oversized hat. It was indeed small, with just four rooms.

'Oh, it is beautiful! You are quite right!' Elizabeth stood delighted.

'Come along, let's look inside.' Mrs Buck pushed them through the door.

'Oh, look! A little fireplace!' said Annie.

'And how quaint, bare wood floors and flowers through the windows. And oh what views!' said Isabella.

'I can see some of the other chalets through this window,' commented George.

'This room shall be where we spend most of our time,' said Elizabeth surveying the largest downstairs room with a table in the centre and another off to one side.

More Love

'Yes, I think so, this is going to be my table,' George said, claiming another one off to the side by putting a case on it, territorially!

'Yes, of course, as long as you don't do too much work at it!' Elizabeth chuckled. The whole family seemed to let out a collective sigh. They had arrived.

On their first day in their new Swiss home they awoke to the sun shining through the window and the breeze seemed to bring with it fresh air and good health. The Prentiss' sat down to their breakfast.

'What is it, Mama?' asked Annie as she watched her siblings shovelling food into their mouths with sticky fingers and greedy smiles.

'It is bread and honey, as you can see!' smiled Elizabeth at her daughter, so used to American breakfasts. 'This is the traditional Swiss breakfast, which you must gobble down quickly as we will miss church if we don't hurry!'

After the service was over they stepped out of the church into the cool Swiss air.

'Well, I didn't understand anything!' Annie said.

'I did understand some sentences. I was quite pleased that my French stretched to that.' Elizabeth had delighted to hear a sermon in another language, the story of God spread worldwide. It was so encouraging to go to another land, somewhere so different to their own, and see the same God was

Elizabeth Prentiss

known and loved here as back at home. God is a big God!

They didn't stay in the chalet for long. Needing more space they moved to a house in Vevay. Elizabeth sat writing letters at the table in the front room whilst the children pottered about around her. Annie was sat holding a tiny little bundle of fur in her hand.

'Annie, be very careful you don't squash it!' Elizabeth warned.

'You can't squash a guinea pig, Mother!' Annie chided.

'I think you'll find that you can, if you are too rough with it,' Elizabeth cautioned again.

'Do you think this guinea pig can speak French?' Annie giggled.

'Well, do you know, I think not only can the guinea pig speak French, but the horses and the dogs too.'

'I wasn't sure I wanted to come to Montreux at all, there aren't really any other children around. But I do like the little girl who lives near us and she was so kind to give us the guinea pigs.' Elizabeth looked at her daughter. She was worried that the young girl was not enjoying herself and the time that she spent with the family. She was rather isolated. However, things had improved now they had moved on from Chateaux d'Oex, their little chalet, to this house in Vevay.

'And,' continued Annie, 'they make lovely cake, and I like the grapes that you can get here.' Elizabeth was

More Love

well aware of her little grape thief who snuck into the kitchen and stole grapes whenever the opportunity allowed.

'And,' Annie carried on, 'I think that Isabella has gone quite mad. I think perhaps the air doesn't agree with her, maybe we are too high up?'

'What do you mean?' Elizabeth had wondered about Isabella herself, although she knew the reason for the madness!

'She mended my shirt and sewed one of the sleeves up so I couldn't get my hand through it!' Annie was aghast.

'Well, dear Annie, one day this kind of madness might happen to you too,' Elizabeth said solemnly.

'What?! Why?'

'Isabella has received some letters from her beau back in America. She,' Elizabeth paused for effect, 'is in love.'

'Ugh, no! Not me. I'm going to hold onto my brain!' Annie declared to Elizabeth's chuckles.

'What are you doing at your table, Mother? You haven't lost your brain and you love Papa. I'm going to be like you.' Annie said, straightening her back up. Elizabeth lay her pen down.

'I am writing letters, my dear, to friends in America who have had their daughter die from an illness.'

'Oh no! That is terrible.' A wave of recognition passed over Annie's face as her young mind was cast back to their own family's sadnesses.

'Yes, it is. But I am using my own experience of your brother and sister to help them. God has given me the chance to write, and write reasonably well, and I have been through these sorrows myself. I shall use my sufferings for the good of others. That is what God calls us to do.'

'I'm not sure I like that. I would rather not have suffered in the first place.'

'I wondered if I thought like that, Annie. But your father and I have decided that we would not change it, even if we could. Your brother and sister are in heaven, they have not had to struggle on in life like we sometimes do. I miss them, but I know that they are better off, and the grief that we felt at their deaths has brought us closer to our Lord Jesus and that is more precious than anything. More than anything.' Elizabeth had tears in her eyes when she turned and looked at her daughter. Would Annie see things the same way?

'Hmm,' Annie mumbled, 'You and Papa are amazing.'

'Minnie!' Elizabeth exclaimed, 'you are not a rabbit! You must not eat quite so much of the lettuce straight out of the garden. We haven't had chance to put it with our dinners.'

Minnie made a crunchy, grumbly noise and spat out a tough bit of stalk.

'Goodness me, Elizabeth, have we got ourselves a feral child?' George looked up from the seat he was perched upon, a book in his lap.

More Love

'I believe that she is not feral just yet, but look how well she is!'

'Yes, and although you have felt unwell with this new one,' George said glancing at his wife's swelling stomach, their next child due soon, 'you do look healthier, I think.'

'As do you, my dear husband. Perhaps we are making some progress.' Elizabeth smiled.

Unfortunately, that progress was somewhat halted over the next period of time.

'The glaciers were the most remarkable thing I have ever seen,' Elizabeth said.

'We have finally been tourists in Switzerland,' George said.

'I feel like I lost my breath just looking at the glaciers. Who could fail to see wonder and majesty and glory of God in those huge pieces of ice?' Elizabeth had been stunned by the entire experience.

'Do you remember when God speaks out of the whirlwind to Job? He tells him that he made all those amazing things on the earth, that he watches the mountain goat that nobody can see, that he opened the fountains of the deep and filled the oceans. That he knows the deep creatures of the sea and the highest birds in the air? It made me really understand all of that,' George said.

'All of that was said to Job as an answer to Job's suffering, wasn't it?' Elizabeth asked George.

Elizabeth Prentiss

'Yes, that's right. Not to explain why it had happened, but to show Job that God holds all of creation in his hands, that he makes order out of chaos, that we need not be afraid of anything because all of our human reason cannot explain what happens in the world always, but it doesn't matter because God is in charge.'

'Just like sometimes we say to the children. Don't worry, and they know not to because they know that we are in charge, and they are not.'

'Yes, I believe that is right,' George said.

In the next few months this was an idea that was going to be extremely useful, as George and Elizabeth stepped over the threshold of the Swiss home, with Annie in tow, after what would be their one and only family tourist trip, to be greeted by a house full of whooping cough.

Elizabeth felt like she had been holding her breath for the entire time since she returned from the glacier. First the new baby, Henry, had succumbed to the frightful illness, then George and Minnie too. The weather was frightfully cold and they had to keep the fires banked in all the rooms in order to steam the children's lungs as much as was possible.

'I fear that Henry is too small to survive this.' Elizabeth said to Isabella. Both women had their hair scraped back off their heads roughly, their sleeves rolled up and pale faces as they rushed to and fro caring for each of the ill children. 'I am sorely afraid that our little

More Love

Swiss boy will be left behind in a little Swiss grave.' Elizabeth gasped with a sob. She buried her head in her apron. Isabella rushed to her side and embraced her firmly.

'No! It will not be, we must keep trying, keep trying!'

By and by the children recovered from whooping cough and although Henry had suffered so much that he barely looked bigger than one of Minnie's dolls he did recover and the household was illness free for a period. Elizabeth was able to make brief excursions to shop for Christmas presents in the nearest town and to visit with friends that she had in the area. By December George had been asked to look after the American chapel in Paris. He had agreed to do so, Elizabeth and the children were to follow him along later.

'I am so very much looking forward to going to Paris,' Annie said to her mother as they pressed flowers amongst the pages of books to hang about the house when they were dry. 'Aren't these daisy ones pretty?' Annie chattered away as they busied themselves.

'It is going to be a good adventure, I am looking forward to it too. We haven't seen much of Switzerland really, what with the babies being unwell.'

'I want to meet some more children my age, there are some who attend the chapel in Paris, the man who asked Papa told him so.'

'That will be a very fine treat...oh goodness, George, whatever is the matter?' Elizabeth cast aside her flowers and stood up as little George stumbled into the room. He wasn't walking properly, his eyes were slightly glazed over and he had a look of fever about him, to Elizabeth's experienced eye. Elizabeth scooped George up into her arms, shocked that his little body radiated heat in a most unnatural way.

'Mother, what is it?' Annie looked anxiously on, her own experience of frequent illnesses in the family telling her that there was something very amiss.

'I think George is quite unwell. Oh my, Papa has only been gone forty-eight hours.'

George was bundled up to bed where his two other young siblings, Minnie and Henry shortly followed. Another bout of illness had struck the Prentiss family, and this was to be a long one.

'Well, surely it is scarlet fever. You are completely confined to the house, you realise, Mrs Prentiss.' The doctor said, adjusting the mask he had placed around his face.

'I understand,' Elizabeth said, on the cusp of despair. Not only for herself but for all of them. George could not return home, not only because of his responsibilities in Paris, but because the house was in quarantine and it would be extremely unwise to put himself at risk of catching the illness. His health was better, but he had been so unwell before. Elizabeth was already exposed, so housemaid, nurse and comforter all fell onto her. Annie was bored and unhappy with the situation. The chance to be in Paris had been whisked away from her, but she never complained. She endured with remarkable grace for a child so young.

Elizabeth showed the doctor out of the house and returned to the downstairs room. She had set up a makeshift bed in the room where Minnie, the worst sufferer, was lying on it. Because she could not bare any light in her eyes, it hurt them so badly, Elizabeth put up a curtain around her bed. It looked somewhat like the bed a Tudor king or queen would have used to keep out the chill. Elizabeth sat right next to it, so that Minnie knew that she was there.

'Mama?' came a sad and poorly little voice from behind the curtain. Elizabeth pulled aside a tiny gap and poked her head through, so as to avoid too much light creeping in, unbidden.

'Yes, sweet angel?' Elizabeth looked at her tiny little daughter, once again too small for her age, ravaged by illness. Elizabeth did not know if she would pull through.

'Drink?' Minnie wanted water. The doctor had advised not to let her gulp down too much at once, for it risked making her sick and then dehydrated, but this did not help Minnie's ravaging thirst.

'You may have a tiny sip, sweetheart, let me hold your head up a little.' Elizabeth carefully supported Minnie's head whilst the child took a sip, reaching

Elizabeth Prentiss

for it with her mouth as Elizabeth reluctantly pulled it away.

'More, Mama!' Minnie groaned.

'In a minute, let that little bit go down first.' Elizabeth stroked her head. Minnie closed her eyes. Elizabeth sighed and returned to writing her letter, her lifeline to the outside world.

A long, slow month passed. The household was still quarantined. Elizabeth wrote another letter to her friend in America:

I believe George has written you about our private hospital. He had not been gone to Paris forty-eight hours when G. was taken sick; that was a month ago, and I have only tasted the air twice in all that time. G. had the disease lightly. M. poor little darling was much sicker than he was. It was a fortnight since she was taken and she hardly sits up at all; an older child would be in bed, but little ones never will give up if they can help it; I suppose it is because they can be held in the arms and rocked, and carried about. I have passed through some most anxious hours on account of M., and it seems little less than a miracle that she is still alive.

The whole thing has been so evidently ordered and planned by God that I have not dared to complain...

The Prentiss', minus their father George, were confined for forty days in one room. This was the treatment required to stop the illness from spreading to other people. This was a hard task for anyone to put up with.

More Love

'Mama, I think the walls are moving towards me.' Annie said, as she stroked the hair on Minnie's head, which lay in her lap.

'I know, but they aren't, it just feels like they are,' Elizabeth said, patiently.

'Why?'

'Because you are looking at them a lot. Let's play a little game, in our little room, how about that?' Elizabeth said, with enforced cheerfulness. 'We have been here twenty days and we need to be here twenty more. That is forty in total, and that is the time that Jesus spent in the wilderness. We shall pretend that that is where we are. What should we have to do to pretend that?'

'We should make sure that we don't turn any rocks into bread?' Annie was a bit confused with this game.

'I'm not sure we will end up doing that! No, perhaps we can remember the things that Jesus said when he was tempted. He knew the scriptures so well that he could answer any question. Can you remember any of it, Annie?'

The two of them sat and recounted, as best they could, all the stories of the Old Testament that testified to who Jesus was, the time passed quickly. For that day, anyway.

Louisa and the War

Elizabeth and the family eventually returned home to America, by way of England and a trip to the sights in London. They returned to home in New York and were greeted well by friends and family who had missed them.

During this time the war of the states was taking place in America. This was a war between the Northern states and the Southern. As with all wars, there were many complicated and sad reasons for their beginning and their prolonged end. One of the main issues that the people fought about was slavery. The Northern states did not support slavery, whilst the Southern states would not agree to abolish it. Elizabeth and George spent a long time thinking and praying about the war and were extremely preoccupied with it, so that there is little writing or letters from that time. However, some sad and troubling events did take place, concerning Elizabeth's sister Louisa.

'Anna has sent us some of these lovely things!' Elizabeth said to her children as they returned home

More Love

from a walk. The children scrambled to see Elizabeth sat amongst all manner of things in their main parlour of the New York house they now lived in. All four of them, much bigger now, bundled into the room, young George knocking over a basket of mending as he went.

'Take care, George!' said Annie.

'It doesn't matter, Annie. Come and see all these treasures.' The children sat around in a makeshift circle admiring all the things that Elizabeth had unpacked from the case that had arrived that morning. There were pine cones, bundles of moss, interesting twigs with patterns and colours on that only the most accomplished tree can produce. There were some pressed flowers, a few sprigs of holly, some purple berries on twigs, a plant that produced a seed that looked like clouds, or perhaps old man's whiskers. All manner of delight that nature could come up with.

'My!' declared Minnie, for all the children shared in their mother's delight at such things. 'What wonderful treasures!'

'I know!' Elizabeth almost squealed with delight. 'I'm going to use some of my wire and make an ornament for your father's study for when he works in there. I might make a display on the mantle piece with some of the holly and berries. It really is quite delightful.'

'Why did Mrs Warner send these things to you, Mama?' Annie enquired, always, as the oldest one, aware of other things that hadn't been mentioned. Elizabeth quietened a bit.

'She knows that I love all these things very much and she also knows how sad I have been, since Louisa died.'

'Why did Aunt Louisa have to die?' Minnie asked, with childlike curiosity, oblivious to her mother's distress. Elizabeth turned sad eyes towards her girl.

'She was called home by our Heavenly Father. She had been poorly for such a long time. Most of her life really.'

'She was worried that she would get really very unwell, wasn't she, Mama?' Annie said.

'Yes, she was quite fearful that if she became much worse, then she might go mad. I think, that perhaps that wasn't very likely, but she was so poorly she couldn't see things clearly.'

'Do you miss her, Mama?' Minnie reached and grasped her mother's hand.

'Yes, terribly, she was my big sister, she was such a wonderful woman, so clever, she wrote such beautiful things, always has done. I will always miss her, but we know, don't we, that we will see her again one day.'

Elizabeth looked around her at the wounded soldiers returning from the war efforts. The war was not over yet and there seemed to be little end to the suffering that some of these men were to endure. She had travelled with Louisa's husband who was endeavouring to help those most injured. 'Will that not be too much medicine, Albert?' Elizabeth queried to her brother-in-law.

More Love

'It is the right amount, it will dull the pain.' Albert said, dully himself.

'Do you think that he shall get home?' Elizabeth bent down to mop the brow of the injured man, regarding his face with surprise as she looked at a mere boy, of only sixteen rather than a man that she expected.

'Not if we do not do something,' Albert said briskly. He waved to a passing medic and issued him with instructions. The medic nodded and rounded up two men to help carry the injured lad towards a waiting wagon. Albert reached down and tucked a piece of paper in the top pocket of the boy's coat.

'What is that?' Elizabeth asked.

'His home address, so that someone sends him to the right place.' Albert said. 'Come on, I've heard we are nearly at the right place.' Albert marched ahead, determinedly but with the stoop of a man ten years older than he was. These few years had aged him terribly, first Louisa and now his son, Eddy also, killed in action in the war. Elizabeth had come with him whilst he investigated how he could find Eddy and bring him home to bury him. They stood in line outside the office of an official-looking man in army fatigues. Elizabeth sincerely hoped that her nephew would be found. She cast her mind back to a few of the girls at church who had been engaged to men who fought in the war. When they returned injured, broken in mind and body, a couple of the girls had broken off the engagement. This had infuriated Elizabeth. She recalled her conversation with George,

'How can they abandon them so? When they are most in need of support?' Elizabeth had raged.

'I know, my dear, I have counselled not, but they are foolish young girls and they don't listen, even to their pastor.' George had sighed and run his hand through his hair, unhappy with the way that things had come about for these poor men.

'I feel hopeless, George. I want to help them.'

'Put pen to paper then. You are most effective at that. Perhaps that will achieve what you fear you cannot do,' George advised.

So that is what Elizabeth did. 'Aunt Jane's Hero' was about a girl called Maggie who could not bear to see that her friends had abandoned their engagement to war heroes. In the end Maggie marries a man called Horace who lost a limb whilst fighting. It felt good to Elizabeth, to have written down her thoughts in this way. She hoped that she would help change the behaviour of some of these women who failed to appreciate the sacrifice that these men had made.

At Home with Lizzie

Elizabeth's days as a pastor's wife allowed her to share some of her experiences in life with the members of the congregation that she and George shared. There were some extremely happy times and some bitterly sad times.

Annie stood at the front of the church, looking only slightly nervous as she looked about her at the sea of faces. She had been a member of a church since she had been born, seventeen years ago, but today was different and all the faces were watching just her. They were friendly faces though, church family, some of them very familiar, others less so, but all of them smiling. Annie's gaze travelled towards the front of the seated congregants to where her family were. She caught eyes with her mother and chuckled. Elizabeth, who sat next to George (which was rare, George was normally leading affairs at the front) was alternatively smiling as if she was the happiest woman on earth and tearing up and dabbing her eyes with her handkerchief. One that she'd embroidered, Annie noticed.

101

More Love

The assistant pastor leant towards her, and asked her in a quiet voice, 'Are you ready, Annie?' Annie nodded. He turned to the rest of the congregation, waving his hands expansively as he spoke.

'Family, we are here today to hear Annie Prentiss' confession of faith and welcome her into the family of God and to this little corner of it in New York.' He reached over to the lectern and picked up a piece of paper. He read from it,

'Annie.' He paused and looked at her before continuing. 'Do you publicly confess that Christ is your Lord and Saviour?'

'Yes, I do,' Annie replied.

'Now you are old enough to make this declaration for yourself, we welcome you to the family of this church and look forward to sharing your walk of faith with you.' The assistant pastor ended with a flourish and the church smiled and some people clapped (some of which Annie noticed came from her younger brothers). She caught eyes with her mother again. The tears had dried on her cheeks. She looked radiant in her happiness. Her sole aim in life was to bring her children up in the faith of the Lord Jesus Christ. All other things were just extras. This was her greatest happiness, to see Annie walking with Christ through her own choice. Not because her parents wanted her to but because Annie believed in Jesus, had his righteousness counted to her and walked with him every day, in a personal relationship with him.

***

The years were passing. Elizabeth's life entered a regular, if busy pattern of pastoral work and assisting George with his work in the church. The children were growing up. There were many bouts of illnesses, but they were endured quite well. Elizabeth's typical day was relentlessly active and varied.

'Goodness, George, do hurry up a bit!' Elizabeth may be older and wiser, but her passion of her younger days still spilled out of her in times of heightened anxiety.

'Don't worry, Lizzie, we aren't going to be late,' her husband said patiently.

'We might be. Your shirt was pressed, your tie is there, all you need to do is put on your jacket and then we can be going.'

'Elizabeth, calm down. You never worry like this usually. Do not let the wealth of these folk intimidate you. They have invited us around to tea because they love us and they want to spend time with us, not to cause you to fly into a state of hysteria!'

'I know, I do know, but I worry what it will look like if we turn up late. I realise that what others think about us is not the most important thing. Even if they think we are the most rude and awful guests for being late, it does not matter, because it is what God thinks of us that is most important. I think I'm forgetting myself in the business of the last few days.'

More Love

'Well said, Lizzie. And only God knows quite what we have to do each day!'

'Only God knows that you were up until quite the middle of the night last night writing a sermon and a lecture,' Elizabeth said, slightly disapprovingly.

'That we'd only just returned the night before from Mr and Mrs Wilson's ball.'

'Oh goodness, that was such a grand affair. I couldn't quite believe it. All those dresses, and the smart ballroom. Can you believe how wealthy some of our congregation are?' Elizabeth was still dazed by that.

'I know. Only God knows that you had spent the previous day with that wee boy and his mother, who was so ill. That you had held her hand as he slipped into the Lord's arms and whispered words of comfort to her in her grief.' George smiled tenderly, only his wife could do what was necessary when the congregation needed that kind of help. The voice of her experience combined with her endless compassion made her the perfect counsellor for those at the worst point in their life.

'Only God knows that you've also had that funeral this morning, poorly attended that it was, and now we must run in haste to our hosts' house if we are to get there in time to take part!'

'And, if past experience reminds me, we must run back home again afterwards to work off all the food that we shall be plied with,' George commented, patting his waistline.

Elizabeth Prentiss

'Oh gosh, yes, last time there were cakes, buns, cheese, fruit, at least three types of puddings and I can't remember what else. It is impossible, with all of that in my stomach to think of the least sensible thing to say,' Elizabeth gasped.

'And, really, the only reason that they have invited us, is not for this luncheon party at all, but because, despite their wealth, they are desperately sad in other ways and want our wise words and counsel,' George said.

'That's right. My plan is to invite Mrs Wilson to our needlework circle. I think the company of other Christian women will be of great encouragement to her. They both need, I believe, to simply be immersed more in the family of God. They have been Christians such a short time, they aren't quite used to the life of it.' Elizabeth stood thinking aloud. George marched past her, swung open the door and called back,

'Well come along then. Otherwise we will be late!' And he ducked as Elizabeth tossed her hat at him and, stopping down to pick it up for her, trotted along the road to their destination.

'Do you know,' Elizabeth said, some time later, 'that I still cannot believe that we have been more than twenty years married?'

'What a life we have had. I'm so glad that I have shared it with you.' George reached for and held onto tightly, his wife's hand. They were sitting on the porch

More Love

swing of the house that they had recently moved into in their favourite summer place of Dorset. Elizabeth and the children would come there for quite a few months in the summer with George joining them when he was available.

'We have seen so much grief,' Elizabeth said. She was thinking not just of Eddy and Bessie but of the many family members that they had lost along the way. Brothers and sisters not just in the family but in God's family too.

'We have seen a good deal of grief. I am grateful to God that we can turn to him for rest for our souls.'

'My soul is weary, as is my body. I am nearly fifty years old!' Elizabeth said rubbing her hands which had felt sore and aching. Elizabeth had tried to keep up with her husband's energy that day. He had pulled up weeds, chopped down bushes, raced about pruning things and putting up fences. It was doing him so much good and satisfying his need for distraction as he worried about yet another ill family member, this time his sister Anna who was grievously ill and would not live long.

'Do you recall, George, the time when I visited Mr and Mrs Greeves'?' Elizabeth asked, in the spirit of reminiscence.

'Yes, I recall quite clearly. That was a horrible tragedy, how that child deteriorated.' George looked grieved all of a sudden.

'I remember that day so well. It started seemingly brightly, I recall that the sun shone beautifully through the leaves on the trees, truly dappled sunlight, like you read about in poetry. I could imagine Wordsworth's England as I looked up that day. I can clearly remember praying, 'Thank you, Lord, for the beauty of your creation, that we marvel at it as the seasons change, as growth and new life and wonder are all around us.' I was very content and thoughtful, especially about the approach of springtime. Anyway, I was aroused at that time, from my meditations by a caller who arrived in some distress to tell me about the poor Greeves child. He had been around to visit not one week earlier and had hopped and skipped about the place with our children. I remember thinking he was like a little puppy, smiling all the time and never sitting still!'

'Just like Henry was,' George commented.

'Exactly. Then the caller arrived to tell me that he had taken ill, and was so suddenly dead. I did not know what to think. Grief just overtook me, I was shocked. I thought of them all, suddenly without their dear child, who had so recently seemed to have life spilling out of him, like springtime was in his bones! Suddenly gone.'

'I'll never forget it. The whole church mourned that day.'

'Yes, but I just didn't know what to do. Should I visit them, I thought, or would I be intruding? Who was I, to step into their life at that moment and suppose that I had something to say that they wanted to hear? I was so conflicted, I so wanted to help.' She paused, reliving the moment of anguish and indecision. 'But I have

More Love

noticed that quite often our need to help sometimes overwhelms the needs of those we are trying to help.'

'You mean, that we sometimes feel their pain so much that we want to *do* something, even if that something isn't actually helpful.'

'Yes, that's it, to fix it. Well, I had been so aware of that, that I was too nervous to visit them in their pain. I wanted to not try and "fix" their problem. Who could fix it? Only God.'

'I remember now,' George said as he pushed the swing chair with one foot to make it go again, 'I remember you saying that to me. My response was…'

'You said,' Elizabeth interrupted, 'that it was true, only God could help them in their time of grief, but how would anyone know that if nobody went to tell them. You said, who better than one who has walked that dark road too?'

'I'm quite poetic when the mood takes me, aren't I?' George chuckled. 'I was right though, you have learnt a great many things about the ways of the Lord, and travelled with him a long time. You were the perfect choice. They were pleased to see you, were they not?'

'Yes, I arrived that day and Mrs Greeves grabbed my arms and fairly pulled me into the house. I thought I'd fall over! She was blotchy eyed and puffy faced and I could see that this was a momentary break in the tears, but oh the warmth of their reception. They were so glad to see me.'

Elizabeth Prentiss

'Because you brought Christ to them, when they could not find him themselves.'

'I truly understood that verse in Galatians about bearing one another's burdens at that moment. I determined that never again would I hesitate from going to those who are in need. I would go, and like you say, take Christ with me. If that was my heart's intentions, then I would never be in the wrong.'

'Well said, dear Elizabeth, well said.' George pushed hard on the swing again and laughed when his wife shrieked and fell backwards.

The family arrived back home from Dorset in October and were watching the autumn return once again. Elizabeth was sat in the parlour gazing out of her window. She was watching the fat little birds boldly hopping around the grass, pulling at this and that, trying to remain fat in the face of approaching wintertime. The most amusing thing about them was that they never sat still, not for a moment, their twitchy, jerky, flapping and bobbing made Elizabeth feel tired simply watching. A person walked past on the street outside and they all flew upwards in a rush, landing in the nearby tree in one mass of wings and tweeting. Then, like children playing a trick on their mother, they snuck back down again, one by one, each following their more brave neighbour until they were back on the grass dancing about like children allowed out on the first day of summer. Elizabeth smiled to herself,

More Love

all throughout her life she had adored God's created world, it made her thankful and aware of his presence all around her. She reflected upon the verse in the Bible that reminded the reader of God's watchful gaze, that even the sparrows are under his attention. Nothing was too little for God to pay attention to it, not even her feathered friends outside.

Stepping Heavenward

In a pique of frustration Elizabeth flung her pen further than she should have. It landed with a crash on the floor. She let out an exasperated huff and collapsed back into her chair. The two ladies who sat across the room engaged in sewing and reading looked up with no small degree of surprise.

One who was wearing a black taffeta gown exclaimed, 'Goodness me, Elizabeth, whatever is the matter with you?'

'I cannot do it. I just cannot. In fact, I will not. It's going in the fire. It's no good.' Elizabeth looked despondent.

'No!' her friend cried, 'I've read a few lines and find it to be quite the best thing you've ever written. Do not stop, and do not throw it on the fire!'

'What is it about, Elizabeth?' asked the other woman who was sitting there.

'It is about a girl called Katy. It is for adults, well, women I expect, although I'm sure it wouldn't matter who read it. Not that they will, I can't finish it.'

More Love

'Nonsense, you must, let us help you. Will you let us read it?' Elizabeth's friend asked, brushing some crumbs off her black sash while the other woman nodded enthusiastically next to her.

'I could do, perhaps I should read it to you?' Elizabeth was uncertain.

'Yes, oh marvellous, do that!' they both exclaimed.

'All right. Tomorrow then.'

Next day Elizabeth visited her friends' room. She poked her head round it and found the two women once again seated, by the window this time, in the midst of conversation. The fire in the grate roared well, but Elizabeth didn't glance at it, she was not going to throw anything in it just yet! She carried in her hands a little green box and said,

'Now you've got to do penance for your sins, you two wicked women!' The other two laughed and one pulled around the other armchair so that Elizabeth could take a seat with them next to the window. Elizabeth took out her papers and began to read the unfinished manuscript.

She told them a story of a woman named Katy. The book began when Katy was still a sixteen-year-old girl, and progressed as she grew up, married and had children. It was a journey of spiritual growth through trials and difficulties, domestic and spiritual. Written as a diary the entries were filled with what Elizabeth's friends described as wisdom and insight, reflected by Elizabeth's own personal life.

Elizabeth Prentiss

Elizabeth drew a deep breath. 'And that,' she said, 'is as far as I've gotten.' She placed her hands in her lap and looked up expectantly. The women burst into a round of applause.

'You are absolutely forbidden to stop,' Elizabeth was told sternly. 'It is truly a wonder this book, it will bless and encourage many. I think that you must carry on. However, I do wonder what you will call it? For it surely cannot continue to be known as 'my Katy story', can it?'

Elizabeth nodded. Her friend was right.

'No, I suspect it cannot! I shall have to give that some thought,' Elizabeth said, looking a lot brighter than she had the previous day. All threats of burning of books evaporated in her mind.

Some time later Elizabeth sat reading a letter when George came into the room.

'What are you reading?' he enquired.

'It is a letter from my publisher. My book is going to be serialised in the Chicago Tribune. They will begin in February.' She looked up excitedly from the letter.

'That's great news, what did you decide to call it, in the end?'

'My friends and I have decided upon 'Stepping Heavenward', like Wordsworth's 'Stepping Westward'. We all agree it is the right name for it.'

'Then I heartily agree too!' George said.

More Love

'Stepping Heavenward' was to become a success. People far and wide read it, and it received a good deal of attention. Elizabeth received many letters from the readers of her books, eager to share their enthusiasm for what they had read with the author.

Elizabeth looked around the group of women that made up her prayer circle. These women faithfully prayed for many things and Elizabeth knew she could trust them to pray with her now.

'I read a letter this morning,' she began, 'it was from a little girl in England.' The ladies looked amazed that Elizabeth's books were read so far away. 'That's not it though, the letter said that the family had read my books for a long time and were very pleased to do so. They associated the Suzy books in particular with their little sister "Pearlie". She taught herself to read from them! She became frightfully ill and still read them, then she lost her ability to speak and by using hand gestures she asked to be baptised like Suzy. The girl writes that eventually "Pearlie" did pass away. I have a photo of her that she sent here.' Elizabeth held it up to show. 'But there is more, the mother never really recovered from the death of her daughter but did always wish she could meet me. She died too. What tragedy! Yet this little girl has taken the time to write to me and to send me their best photo of "Pearlie". I wish for us to pray for them, if we can?' There was no objection from the group as they all bowed their heads and lifted that family and that little girl up to the Lord in prayer.

* * *

Another day Elizabeth strode into the kitchen at home and found the boys once again eating.

'Are you boys still hungry?' Elizabeth said, amused. They were growing into strapping lads and apparently needed to eat hourly to maintain this upward trajectory!

'Don't answer!' Elizabeth declared, 'your mouths are too full!' Elizabeth reached into her pocket and pulled out another letter she had read just that morning. 'Would you like to hear this letter I've gotten about my book?' She asked, hopefully. Henry, who had swallowed down the last crumb of fruit cake spoke first.

'Yes, absolutely, is it another one from a girl somewhere?'

'No, this one is from a woman. She had lost a child and her husband had an accident at work, he lost his leg.'

'Oh, how awful' said the younger George.

'Quite, she writes that my book was such an encouragement to her. She was close to despair, but then she read it and she knew that she was not to give up. She knew that she was not alone, and that a lot of women went through the pain and suffering that she was going through and became closer to God as a result.'

'That's brilliant, Mother!' said Henry.

'Yes, well done, Mama, you are clever!' George concurred.

'Not I, but Christ in me!' Elizabeth said.

More Love

Elizabeth gave a little sigh and picked up her pen once more. She was always writing letters, her entire life had been a long series of correspondences with friends and family, but now she wrote to Annie. Annie was away, in Europe, for a whole year. She was to travel with some family friends and would even go back to Switzerland and see some of the places that they had stayed all those years before. But, oh, did Elizabeth miss her! It was not simply that Annie had been educating the younger children, allowing Elizabeth to attend to her duties as a pastor's wife, not at all. Annie was in the very fabric of the house, a dearly loved companion, daughter and wise counsel. Elizabeth had loved to see her grow into the wonderful, faithful woman she had become. She delighted that, despite all her parents' failing, Annie had developed into not only a marvellous young lady, as society would see it, but a faithful servant of Christ. So much more important! Elizabeth wrote about her day to day adventures and interests, keeping Annie abreast of news and titbits about her siblings. It was the passing of the minutiae of life that was so important to families and what made such a difference to whether one felt wanted and loved or not. She wrote about all the visits that she made but also of all the people who came to the house seeking the support and love of George and Elizabeth. George had suggested they erect a sign outside that read '*souls cured here*' to indicate where people could come for spiritual guidance. Annie would laugh at that! It had taken a reasonable amount

Elizabeth Prentiss

of persuasion to stop Henry and George from going outside and finding their woodwork tools to make the sign! Elizabeth was content. She knew that if she did nothing more for the rest of her life than visit those who suffered and needed help she would be utterly fulfilled and would rejoice. Showing Christ and what he could be to such people if they would allow it was her profound interest. She was so pleased to have the opportunities.

Joy in the Hard Times

Elizabeth, buoyed by her success, went on to write a good deal more books for children and adults. She would continue to act as a pastor's wife and support those who needed her until George resigned his position to take up a teaching post in Chicago. This proved to be a big change for Elizabeth, one that left her no longer in the role she was used to. Yet, she continued on, desiring to make sure that every day she did something that she could identify as serving the Lord.

Life continued in this way for sometime. However, Elizabeth, as she grew older, began to long to see her Father face to face. She wished to be reunited with her children who had died before her. One week she spent quite ill. She was taken to bed and remained there. George fretted and worried about her, praying earnestly for her and for her health. He sat with her in her room, in the armchair pulled up closely so that he could offer her water and sips of beef tea when she needed it. Elizabeth opened her eyes from the lying position in the bed and looked at him calmly.

More Love

'*Darling, don't you think you could ask the Lord to let me go?*' George choked back on a sob and Elizabeth tried her best to explain her earnest desire to go to Christ, that she wished to not be apart from him anymore. George understood. Elizabeth's wishes were not put off much longer. On a beautiful, sunny day, one which would usually delight Elizabeth, all the family gathered around her bed. The girls were crying quietly and the boys were stoic but burdened. Surrounded by her family Elizabeth passed from this life and went to be with her Heavenly Father as was her desire. Elizabeth went on to the Lord at the age of fifty-nine, in 1878.

After Elizabeth died the family mourned her for a long time. George Prentiss wrote later that he would feel terribly lonely at points in the year. That he missed her always. George lived to an impressive age of eighty-seven. He and the family still met for frequent summers at the Dorset house.

'Father, are you quite ninety yet?' Henry joked.

'My boy, I am a sprightly eighty-six and I will thank you to not mention it!' George smiled at his 'Swiss boy' as Elizabeth had called him. All grown up. Married to the lovely Lila. In charge of his own company. There was a flurry of noise, little feet and a bark. First appeared a dog, his tongue trailing out of the side of his mouth and his tail wagging so hard it banged the walls and doors. Next followed three girls, all remarkably similar, dresses tucked in their undergarments and hair trailing out behind them.

'Girls! You look quite feral!' Annie, their mother chastised them.

'I remember you children turning to the wild when you were all younger,' George commented, reminiscing.

'What did Mama think of that?' Annie asked.

'Oh, she was always so happy with you all, you were delightful. She enjoyed watching you have your fun.' George would have carried on, but the remainder of the noise appeared in the form of two younger girls looking slightly tidier if only because they couldn't keep up with their cousins.

'Ha!' said Henry, 'that's my girls, you still look reasonable, even if you are trailing your reprobate cousins around!' Annie huffed at that, but smiled at the two little girls indulgently.

'Ah, I am so glad to have my family around me.' George sat in his chair, with a rug over his lap. 'Your mother always was delighted when all the family were around her.'

'She was an amazing woman,' said Annie.

'An amazing writer,' Henry said.

'Yes, but she always told me that her first calling was not to writing but to being a wife and mother,' Minnie said.

'Yes,' George answered. 'That's right. That was always her main calling, after serving Christ.'

'Exactly, and she taught us and so many others so much about him!' finished Annie.

Thinking Further Topics

A Girl Called Lizzie

Lizzie grew up in a very happy and warm family. However, very early on she experienced a tragedy, her father died. After this time she decided that she would pray frequently.

Do you ever pray? Have you thought about prayer? In the Bible the disciples ask Jesus about prayer. He tells them that when they pray they should pray like this:

'And when you pray, you must not be like the hypocrites. For they love to stand and pray in the synagogues and at the street corners, that they may be seen by others. Truly, I say to you, they have received their reward.

But when you pray, go into your room and shut the door and pray to your Father who is in secret. And your Father who sees in secret will reward you.

"And when you pray, do not heap up empty phrases as the Gentiles do, for they think that they will be heard for their many words.

Do not be like them, for your Father knows what you need before you ask him.

Pray then like this:

Our Father in heaven, hallowed be your name.
Your kingdom come, your will be done, on earth as it is in heaven.
Give us this day our daily bread,

and forgive us our debts, as we also have forgiven our debtors. And lead us not into temptation, but deliver us from evil."
(Matthew 6:5-13)

Here Jesus tells us a few things that are important about prayer.

- He tells us not to perform it for other people to think well of us. Do it for God only.
- Prayers don't have to be long to be good!
- That when we pray we can say 'Father' because God is our father. That is important, it shows that we are important to God and that he wants to know us, and to know us by talking with us. How many friends do you have that you don't speak to? Not many! Spending time with God is the way to build a relationship with him.

Thinking about all of this changes how we 'do' praying. Praying is like having a talk with God. It is not something that must be performed, although sometimes we do pray out loud for others to join in with. It is something that comes from wanting to spend time with God.

Challenge: Can you spend more time talking to God? Can you find a time that you can regularly talk to God in? It could be before you go to sleep, or when you get up in the morning, or both?

Growing up with Christ

Elizabeth decided that one thing that she would like to do was to learn a catechism. A catechism is an old way of remembering true things about God and all that he has told us about him and us. Here is an example of a catechism.

Q. What do you believe when you say,
'I believe in God, the Father almighty, creator of heaven and earth'?

A. That the eternal Father of our Lord Jesus Christ,
who out of nothing created heaven and earth
and everything in them,[1]
who still upholds and rules them
by his eternal counsel and providence,[2]
is my God and Father
because of Christ the Son.
I trust God so much that I do not doubt
he will provide
whatever I need
for body and soul,[4]
and will turn to my good
whatever adversity he sends upon me
in this sad world

God is able to do this because he is almighty God and desires to do this because he is a faithful Father

This is from the Heidelberg Catechism. The language is quite old, but the questions and answers are all based on the Bible. People would, and still do, memorise the catechism so that all through their day they would be able to recall things about God. It helped them grow closer to God each day.

In the Bible God tells the Israelites to speak to their children all the time about him, in Deuteronomy 6:7 it says:

'You shall teach them diligently to your children, and shall talk of them when you sit in your house, and when you walk by the way, and when you lie down, and when you rise.'

God is telling parents to talk to their children about his law all the time, so that they remember it.

Challenge: You might like to learn a catechism. There are ones available for children, or you can use an adult one! Or, you might like to try and memorise verses from the Bible. What can you do to help your knowledge of God?

Teaching the Girls in Richmond

When Elizabeth taught the girls in Richmond she would rise really early in the morning to pray. She carved out time when she might have preferred to be in bed! Jesus showed us how to do this. He went into the wilderness for forty days to spend time with God the Father. This shows that praying is important and something that we should put high up on our list of things to do.

Elizabeth also spent time with two girls at the school. They both had different needs that she sought to help. She did this because Jesus asked people:

'Truly, I say to you, as you did it to one of the least of these my brothers, you did it to me' (Matthew 25:40).

By this Jesus meant that when we look after people who may not seem like they are important, we are actually doing it as if they were God himself. God values everyone, not just special people, and we should value everyone too, just like he does and serve them as if we were serving God himself.

Challenge: How can you make time to pray? Is there something that you might need to give up to make time? Could you turn off the TV earlier? Could you wake up a bit sooner?

How are you serving 'the least of these'? Is there somebody at school who is not very popular? Do you stop and help when little ones fall over at the park? Who are the 'least of these' in your life?

Blessings and Sadness

Elizabeth endured the death of two of her children. This is an awful thing. Later on in her life she looked back at this time and said that it was a time she drew closer to the Lord and got to know him better. How can this be? In the Bible Job suffers in a similar way. He asks his friends to help him and they give him lots of long reasons why the bad things might have happened. In the end, when they haven't really helped, God himself speaks. This is an example of what God says:

'Have you commanded the morning since your days began, and caused the dawn to know its place' (Job 38:12).

You might think, what has that got to do with how sad Job is? Well the answer is this: God answered Job by saying, are you in charge? Do you know how all the animals are made? Do you keep the world turning around and making sure that everything is happening as it should? God was showing Job that no matter what, God is in charge. Things do sometimes go wrong, and sometimes very badly, but God knows about it and he cares. He cares about the mountain goats, it says in Job, whom nobody else can see, and he cares about us.

In the story of Elijah we hear about how, after working really hard, Elijah is exhausted. He even asks to die. God meets with him:

'But he himself went a day's journey into the wilderness and came and sat down under a broom tree. And he asked that he might die, saying, "It is enough; now, O LORD, take away my life, for I am no better than my fathers."

And he lay down and slept under a broom tree. And behold, an angel touched him and said to him, "Arise and eat."

And he looked, and behold, there was at his head a cake baked on hot stones and a jar of water. And he ate and drank and lay down again.

And the angel of the LORD came again a second time and touched him and said, "Arise and eat, for the journey is too great for you."

And he arose and ate and drank, and went in the strength of that food forty days and forty nights to Horeb, the mount of God' (1 Kings 19:4-8).

God looks after Elijah and tells him to rest. Even though Elijah has reached a point of despair, God cares and helps him.

Challenge: You may have had some hard things happen to you. Can you pray to God about them and ask for his comfort and his help?

Writing, Writing, Writing

Elizabeth from a very young age wrote things. She wrote stories, poems and letters. She wrote to encourage others and also to express herself. Sometimes her writings were full of sadness and anger, other times hope and joy.

Challenge: Can you write a poem or a letter? It could be for someone else to read, or it could be just for you.

Letters and holidays

Annie and Elizabeth helped a little girl who was very poor. She and her family had not enough to eat and no useful clothes to wear. Jesus asked his followers to look after the poor:

'For I was hungry and you gave me food, I was thirsty and you gave me drink, I was a stranger and you welcomed me,

I was naked and you clothed me, I was sick and you visited me, I was in prison and you came to me.'

Then the righteous will answer him, saying, "Lord, when did we see you hungry and feed you, or thirsty and give you drink?

And when did we see you a stranger and welcome you, or naked and clothe you?

And when did we see you sick or in prison and visit you?"

And the King will answer them, "Truly, I say to you, as you did it to one of the least of these my brothers, you did it to me"' (Matthew 25:35-40).

Challenge: Sometimes it is hard to know how to help the poor. Can you think of something you can do? Can you donate some food to a food bank? Could you give your old clothes and toys away to someone who needs them? Can your family sponsor a child abroad who needs help? There are many programmes that you can join in with.

Life in Switzerland

After a while visiting Switzerland the Prentiss family were due to follow George to Paris. Annie was especially excited about this because she had spent a long time without friends her age. However, the rest of the children were taken ill with scarlet fever and instead of going to Paris the family were shut up in one room for a couple of months. Annie was very disappointed but behaved really well. She did not complain and Elizabeth was amazed by her attitude despite the hardships that she was enduring.

Challenge: Can you think of a time when you were really disappointed? Can you remember how you reacted? Sometimes it is very hard not to be cross, angry or upset when things don't go the way we had hoped or planned. Next time you are faced with a disappointment, perhaps you could pray this prayer:

Dear God,
I'm sorry for the way that I have reacted in the past when I have been disappointed. Thank you that you forgive us when we do things wrong. Please help me now, I am feeling like things aren't what I had hoped for or wanted. Please help me to be patient, kind, understanding and to turn to you when I am finding that hard. Amen

Louisa and the war

War is a terrible thing. Elizabeth and George were very concerned about the war and spent a good deal of time praying about it. Elizabeth was also extremely bothered by the treatment of injured soldiers. She wrote a book about a woman who married an amputee. She was concerned that these men were treated badly because they had terrible injuries.

Challenge: How does this relate to your life? It may not be that you know people with war injuries, but do you know someone who looks different? Perhaps they have a physical disability? Do you treat them the same as other people? Do you help them if they need help?

At home with Lizzie

Elizabeth and George had to spend a lot of time with people who were in their congregation at church and were very rich. They went to amazing dances and banquets and saw a great many expensive things.

The Bible says lots of things about money. Jesus says:

'No one can serve two masters, for either he will hate the one and love the other, or he will be devoted to the one and despise the other. You cannot serve God and money' (Matthew 6:24).

Jesus is not telling his listeners to be poor, although sometimes he tells them to give away his money, he means that money should not control us. If we have lots of money or hardly any it should not occupy our thoughts. Money should not be a god to us, God should be!

Challenge: It can be very hard to think well about money. Today there are lots of adverts all around for toys, clothes, cars and things that we can buy. At birthdays and Christmas we think about the things that we might get. As we grow up we start to think about how we can earn money. Toys, clothes, cars and money are not bad things, but they are bad if we let the want of them control us. Maybe you could pray this prayer:

Dear God,
Please help me to put you first in all things. Thank you that you are generous and want us to have good things, help me to see the good things that you have already given me. Please help me not to spend my time always thinking about what I want but to be thankful for the wonderful blessings around me. Amen.

Stepping Heavenward

Elizabeth wrote a lot of books. She used them to tell other people about God and how to get to know him better. She did this all the while raising a family and serving in her church. Sometimes she found the work she did at home, cleaning and cooking and domestic chores, boring. But during that time she wrote amazing things that helped other people. Elizabeth is a good example of being a witness about Jesus from the situation that she was in. She did not go and travel the world to tell people about Jesus, she did not do something impossible or very big. She simply used her gifts and reached out as she felt led by God.

Challenge: Sometimes it can feel like we are small and not very important. It can feel like we don't have anything that we can do for God. However, we can serve God from the place that we are. It might be in a small way, by deciding to help in our house a bit more, or a slightly bigger way, like telling our friends about Jesus or an even bigger way, by deciding to use our God-given talents to serve God our whole lives.

Try and think of a small, a bigger and a biggest way you can serve God.

Joy in the hard times
Elizabeth's family loved her and she loved them. When she died they were very sad. However, they were also very thankful for all that she had done for them. She left behind four children who had learnt about God from her.

Challenge: Who has taught you about God? It might be your parents, or someone at school or church? Thank God for them and all they have taught you.

Elizabeth Prentiss Timeline

26th October, 1818	Elizabeth born in Portland, Maine.
October 1827	Elizabeth's father dies.
May 1831	Elizabeth tells the church she believes that Jesus saves her from her sins and joins the church.
1840–1843	Elizabeth teaches the girls in Richmond, Virginia.
16th April, 1845	Marries George Prentiss.
4th December, 1846	Annie is born.
22nd October, 1848	Eddy is born.
1851	Elizabeth and her family move to New York for George to become a pastor.
16th January, 1852	Elizabeth's son, Eddy, dies.
17th April, 1852	Bessie is born.
19th May, 1852	Elizabeth's daughter, Bessie, dies.
1853	Elizabeth's first book is published – *Little Susy's Six Birthdays*.
23rd July, 1854	Minnie is born.
August 1857	George, named after his father, is born.
April 1858	The Prentiss family leave to travel to Europe.

July 1859	Henry is born, in Switzerland.
1860	Travels to London and other parts of the U.K.
September 1860	The family return to New York.
1861–1865	American Civil War.
1864	Annie joins the church.
1869	*Stepping Heavenward* is published.
1875	Minnie is very ill.
13th August, 1878	Elizabeth dies.

Do the Next Thing: Elisabeth Elliot

by Selah Helms

- The story of an inspirational woman
- Courage in the face of grief
- Part of the Trailblazers biography series
-

Although she is best known for her time on the mission field in Ecuador, Elisabeth Elliot went on to become a vibrant role model for valiant, godly women all over the world. Follow her journey from the jungles of the Amazon, where she faced the tragic death of her first husband, to the lecture halls and radio shows of the culture wars, where she stood as a strong defender of God's Word.

ISBN: 978-1-5271-0161-6

OTHER BOOKS IN THE TRAIL BLAZERS SERIES

Augustine, The Truth Seeker
ISBN 978-1-78191-296-6
John Calvin, After Darkness Light
ISBN 978-1-78191-550-9
Fanny Crosby, The Blind Girl's Song
ISBN 978-1-78191-163-1
John Knox, The Sharpened Sword
ISBN 978-1-78191-057-3
Eric Liddell, Finish the Race
ISBN 978-1-84550-590-5
Martin Luther, Reformation Fire
ISBN 978-1-78191-521-9
Robert Moffat, Africa's Brave Heart
ISBN 978-1-84550-715-2
D.L. Moody, One Devoted Man
ISBN 978-1-78191-676-6
Mary of Orange, At the Mercy of Kings
ISBN 978-1-84550-818-0
Patrick of Ireland: The Boy who Forgave
ISBN: 978-1-78191-677-3
John Stott, The Humble Leader
ISBN 978-1-84550-787-9
Ulrich Zwingli, Shepherd Warrior
ISBN 978-1-78191-803-6

For a full list of Trail Blazers, please see our website: www.christianfocus.com
All Trail Blazers are available as e-books

TRAIL BLAZERS

• Wilfred Grenfell •
COURAGEOUS DOCTOR

Linda Finlayson

Courageous Doctor: Wilfred Grenfell

by Linda Finlayson

"Faster, Jack, faster!" Wilfred Grenfell called to the lead dog in his sledge team. Jack needed no second reminder. He loved to go as fast as possible and he urged his team forward. Wilfred loved to go fast too, and felt a thrill as the cold wind blew past his face. There was such freedom flying across deep snow and ice, and so far, all seemed to be going well. But just then, instead of hard ice, they hit slush, which meant a patch of ice was melting and could break apart at any moment. "Come on Jack," Wilfred yelled. "Faster!" But it did not matter. The worst thing happened. Right in front of the dogs the ice cracked open. Watching in horror, Jack and then one by one the other dogs, slid into the freezing water...

ISBN:978 1 5271 0173-9

TRAILBLAZERS

• David Brainerd •
A LOVE FOR THE LOST

Brian H. Cosby

A Love for the Lost: David Brainerd

by Brian H. Cosby

Life on the American frontier in the early 1700s was very difficult - continually threatened by disease, attack, and brutally cold winters. The English and Native Americans lived side by side, which often led to conflict. David Brainerd arose as a compassionate and fearless missionary to the various Indian tribes in America. Riding on his horse across rivers, over mountains, and through towns, Brainerd carried the gospel of Jesus Christ to the lost, the hurting, and the broken. Notable pastors and missionaries like John Wesley, William Carey, Adoniram Judson and Jim Elliot were all influenced by the life, passion, and dedication of David Brainerd. In this book, Brian Cosby takes the reader on a journey from Brainerd's teenage years on the farm to his expulsion from Yale; from preaching on the frontier to his death in his late 20s. The reader will be encouraged, inspired, and challenged by the perseverance and single-minded devotion of the early American missionary to the Indians, David Brainerd.

ISBN: 978-1-84550-695-7

TRAIL BLAZERS

• Isobel Kuhn •
LIGHTS IN LISULAND

Irene Howat

Lights in Lisuland: Isobel Kuhn

by Irene Howat

Isobel Kuhn wasn't always a missionary — she wasn't always a Christian.

Her teachers discouraged a belief in God and promoted evolution. Isobel sometimes doubted whether there was anybody there at all to hear her prayers. "They don't go beyond the ceiling you know," she once said to her father who was desperately praying for his young daughter.

Isobel even considered suicide once but the thought of her parents' heartache stopped her.

Discover what brought this questioning, antagonistic teenager from doubts to faith in Christ. Find out how she affected the lives of countless people on the mission field of China and Thailand.

This stirring and challenging story of faith is a role model to young people everywhere.

ISBN: 978-1-85792-610-1

CHRISTIAN FOCUS PUBLICATIONS

Christian Focus | Christian Heritage | CF4K | Mentor

Christian Focus Publications publishes books for adults and children under its four main imprints: Christian Focus, CF4K, Mentor and Christian Heritage. Our books reflect our conviction that God's Word is reliable and Jesus is the way to know him, and live for ever with him.

Our children's publication list includes a Sunday School curriculum that covers pre-school to early teens, and puzzle and activity books. We also publish personal and family devotional titles, biographies and inspirational stories that children will love.

If you are looking for quality Bible teaching for children then we have an excellent range of Bible stories and age-specific theological books.

From pre-school board books to teenage apologetics, we have it covered!

Find us at our web page:
www.christianfocus.com

CF4•K
Because you're never too young to know Jesus